A Concise Guide to Taxes in Retirement

Bruce Larsen

ISBN:
ISBN-13: 978-0-9981554-1-8
ISBN-10: 0998155411

DEDICATION

This book is dedicated to the clients I have had the pleasure to work with.

Contents

ACKNOWLEDGEMENTS

I have worked with several outstanding CPAs and Enrolled Agents over my financial planning career. The tax insight I have received from them has greatly expanded my knowledge of the tax scenarios faced by my retired clients.

I want to give special thanks to John Dundon, EA, past President of the Colorado Society of Enrolled Agents. John took on the daunting task of checking the tax calculations throughout the examples in this book.

FOREWORD

The new tax bill that passed at the end of 2017, and become effective for 2018, added a new level of complexity to tax planning. While changes in tax law are faily easy to deal with, the fact that all of the provisions of the new law will sunset in 2025 and we will return to prior law for individual tax payers. In my 2018 update to this book, nearly every example I update resulted in less taxes. We don't know if current law will be extended past 2025 to to be conservative I am assuming we will revert to old tax law without re-authorization.

Just like during our working years, taxes may well be one of our largest budget items when we enter retirement. Tax decisions can have a large impact on our discretionary cash flow for the twenty to thirty years we will spend in retirement.

The intent of the chapters that follow is to provide a guide to those close to, or in retirement, on the tax issues they need to be aware of.

Planning prior to retirement can dramatically change tax rates applicable to our assets for its duration. During our working years we have a much broader array of choices regarding our income; we can get more education to improve our earnings, we can move to a better paying position if available, or we can increase our savings rate. Once retirement starts, our range of choice narrows—we must work with the the benefits we have and savings and investments we have accumulated.

Have you ever met with your tax preparer after your return has been completed and learned that, had you done something different, your taxes would have been lower? Knowing how decisions you make will affect your tax status in advance is a much better approach.

The tax code is very complex. The most routine financial decisions could trigger a cascade of unforeseen harmful effects on your final tax bill. But the code is relatively fixed. It rewards diligence. With timely diligence errors can be avoided.

This book is not a substitute for competent tax advice from a tax professional. It should, howver, provide you with the baseline knowledge you will need to make tax-smart decisions as you enter retirement.

Planning a successful retirement typically takes a team of diverse professionals. Your financial advisor/planner should work with your estate attorney; and your tax professional should have open dialogue with your financial advisor and you. I strongly suggest you have your retirement plan reviewed by your tax professional prior to implementing the recommendations of your financial planner. As a financial advisor, I am not licensed to give tax advice—only a licensed tax professional can do that.

Chapter 1 – Introduction

Anyone who has ever struggled to complete an IRS tax return on time knows that the tax codes are very complex. Were one book to encompass the entire range of topics pertaining to retirees, it would fail both in focus and amplification. This book is intended for retirees needing between $60,000 and $160,000 in net after-tax cash flow in retirement. This profile covers roughly one half of retirees in the United States, with the top 10% to 12% of earners left out. The assumption is that the top income earners have tax advisors in place to help them plan their retirement income. Earners of income in retirement under $60,000 per year will likely have no federal taxes due—further assuming those in this demographic receive total annual Social Security benefits of $44,000 per year with the balance of their income from pensions, taxable IRA distributions, or other taxable income.

Before we get into the details of strategies to reduce the amount of taxes you will pay throughout your retirement, let's take a look at a typical couple's tax circumstances before they retire and then after they collect their gold watches.

Typical Retirement Planning

Bill and Julie Lesley are both 66. They feel they should be able to retire. Both of their children have good jobs, and they are confident that they won't have to provide any further support for the children, although they are considering helping their grandkids with college.

Bill and Julie were fortunate that they didn't have any major financial traumas throughout their careers. Bill was a banker for his entire career. Julie worked as a paralegal at a law firm and stayed with the same group of attorneys for the last 20 years. Both of their incomes were relatively level throughout their careers, increasing at about the same rate as general inflation.

Realizing that retirement saving is important, the Lesleys always tried to make it a priority. Like most couples there were times when they had to put their retirement savings on hold temporarily. It is not uncommon for most of us to need to help our kids for college, remodel our house or any number of other temporary high expenses. For the past five years they both increased their 401(k) contributions to 10% of their salary. They also set a goal to have their home mortgage paid off by age 66.

Working through their retirement projection, they determine that they would like to have about the same in net income as they have now. In other words, they don't want a "pay cut," if possible, once their retirement starts. Bill mentions that he read somewhere that the two greatest cash flow obstacles retirees face are inflation and taxes.

While they realize that nobody can accurately predict inflation, they feel they should be able to determine how much they will pay in taxes. They put together their last year-end pay stubs and develop the chart below.

Bill and Julie Taxes While Working	
Bill's Salary	60,000.00
Julie's Salary	60,000.00
Total Earnings	120,000.00
Health Insurance Premiums	(3,120.00)
401(k) Contributions	(12,000.00)
Gross Income	104,880.00
Standard Deduction	(26,600.00)
Personal Exemptions	-
Federal Taxable Income	78,280.00
Federal Income Taxes	(9,101.00) 8.7%
FICA/Medicare Withholding	(9,180.00)
Net Take-home Pay	86,599.00

Bill and Julie have an effective rate on gross income of 8.7%—not too bad. They assume that because their goal is the same net take home pay that they have now that their taxes in retirement will be about the same. They are unsure whether they will have to pay any Federal Insurance Contribution Act (FICA) and Medicare taxes in retirement. They do an internet search and determine that FICA/Medicare taxes only apply to wages and self-employment earnings. They are pleased that they won't have to pay this in retirement because it is almost as much as they are currently paying in federal taxes.

Assuming Bill and Julie earned about the same salary over their careers adjusted for inflation, their monthly Social Security benefits at their full retirement age of 66 would be about $2,096 each. If they can delay their benefits until 70, which we will see in the next chapter most people should do if they possibly can, their monthly benefits would be $2,766.83 each ($33,201.90 annually).

The Lesleys have combined 401(k) balances of $636,000. They are expecting a long-term return of 7%. Knowing that they will need to increase their income due to inflation, they decide they should limit their withdrawals to 4% of the balance, leaving 3% to reinvest to grow the balance. Four percent of the $636,000 balance equals $25,440.00. They determine that their combined Social Security benefits at 66 are $50,304.00. They add the two numbers together and get to $75,744.00. They then deduct 8.7% for taxes and see that they have net income of $69,154.27. This is $17,444.73 short of their goal of $86,599.00.

Bill and Julie also have savings of $180,000 but they realize if they take the $17,444.73 out of their savings each year, the savings balance will be depleted in about ten years—then where will they be? They decide they will have to wait a few years to retire.

When they tell their son, Bob, that they can't retire, he is surprised. Bob knows that they had always been good savers and had encouraged Bob and his sister to develop the habit of saving. Bob tells them that before they make the decision they should meet with his financial advisor. Bill and Julie think it is probably a waste of time, but they agree to the meeting since the advisor is a friend of Bob's.

Bill and Julie gather up their Social Security statements, their 401(k) account statements, and the print-out of the worksheet they developed that led them to the decision to delay retirement. On the way to the meeting, they are both apprehensive about meeting with Pam, the financial advisor, primarily because they are embarrassed that they will have to admit that they missed their goal of being able to retire at 66.

"I thought we were doing everything right, and it looks like we missed it by a mile," Bill says.

"I don't see how we could have saved more and still have been able to enjoy life along the way," Julie replies.

Pam, having dealt with hundreds of retirees over her career, is not surprised at their apprehension. After assuring them that all information she reviews is confidential, she asks to look at their Social Security statements, their 401(k) statements and their projection spreadsheet.

Pam's first comment is, "Did you realize that if you delay your Social Security until age 70, your benefits will increase by 32 percent?"

Bill says he understands that, but, assuming they retire at 66, they don't want to reduce the principal balances of their savings and 401(k)s to wait until 70. Pam also asks them if they realize that a portion of their Social Security will be excluded from income. They didn't know this. Bill and Julie share a look between each other—both see a glimmer of hope.

Pam says, "Bear with me for a few minutes. Some of what I'm going to say may initially feel uncomfortable, but will you hear me out?" The Lesleys agree they will keep an open mind.

Pam tells them that because Social Security has cost of living adjustments, it makes sense to get as much as they can out of their Social Security benefits so they can partially offset inflation. Pam does a quick calculation, multiplying the $86,599.00 income goal by the four years until they can get maximum Social Security benefits.

Pam says, "To retire now and delay Social Security until 70, we need to come up with $346,396. This amount is not adjusted for inflation; I'll do that when we prepare a formal plan—provided you want me to continue down this road with you." The Lesleys both nod, somewhat tentatively.

Pam says, "Let's take $60,000 of it out of the 401(k)s and the rest out of savings. I know that isn't where you want to go, but bear with me." Pam brings up her tax calculator and enters the $60,000 IRA distribution.

Pam says, "Your taxes over the next four years will only be about $3,735. The savings withdrawal isn't taxable so if we take $26,599 out of savings, plus the $3,735 to pay the taxes we get you there." Pam continues, "This will bring your savings balance down to about $58,000, which I know is uncomfortable, but bear with me." Pam punches some numbers in her financial calculator and says, "Your 401(k) total balance will be down to about $546,000 at age 70, assuming you get your projected 7 percent return."

Bill says, "None of this is sounding very encouraging."

Pam says, "Yes, I understand that. Now let's look at your situation moving forward once you are both 70." Pam works up a quick spreadsheet, again consulting her tax calculation software.

Pam says, "Here is a rough draft of what your scenario will be going forward from age 70 on." Pam turns her computer screen around to show the Lesleys the chart below.

Bill and Julie Taxes at Retirement (age 70)	
Bill's Social Security	33,201.00
Julie's Social Security	33,201.00
Total Social Security	66,402.00
Excluded Social Security	(51,722.00)
Taxable Social Security	14,682.00
IRA Distributions	21,010.00
Gross Income	35,692.00
Standard Deduction	(26,600.00)
Personal Exemptions	-
Federal Taxable Income	9,092.00
Federal Income Taxes	(909.20) 4.3%
Net Take-home Pay	86,502.80

Bill, being a financial guy, looks at the bottom line and says dubiously, "I don't see how our taxes can possibly be that low. We are paying over $9,000 in federal taxes while working."

Pam points to the "Excluded Social Security" line. "The magic is right here. $51,722 of your Social Security benefits are excluded from your income." Pam goes through a brief description of how taxation of benefits works.

Julie says, "So, we can really retire now?"

"I don't see anything stopping you," says Pam.

Pam then tells them that, with their permission, she will prepare a formal retirement plan for them. She tells them there are multiple variables to consider towards generating the cash flow they need. All the variables necessitate an accurate estimate of taxes.

While this is a low tax bill, Pam explains the federal income tax system is set up based on a near-certain guarantee that Bill and Julie will be paying more in tax each year of their retirement as their income increases due to Social Security cost of living adjustments, as well as increases in required minimum distributions from their 401(k)s. We will get into this in more detail later.

Conclusion

Almost all individuals and couples will see a dramatic change in their tax status once they retire. Assumptions based on taxes while working go out the window once you transition from wages and/or self-employment income to pension, Social Security, distributions from tax-deferred accounts and other retirement cash flows. Good retirement planning simply cannot be accomplished without a thorough understanding of the annual tax bill for each and every year of retirement. Understanding retirement taxes can drive strategies that can often significantly improve one's lifetime retirement cash flow.

CHAPTER 2 – Taxation of Social Security

The Social Security system has been in a constant state of change from the very beginning. While it was never intended to provide all of the income needed for a comfortable retirement, it does comprise a significant portion of most retirees' cash flows. Most of the plans I prepare, even for high net worth couples, would not be achievable without the help of Social Security.

When the system began, two revenue rulings from the IRS, one in 1938 and another in 1941, explicitly excluded Social Security benefits from taxation. See—the IRS isn't all bad. This, and IRS magnanimity, changed radically with the passage of the 1983 Amendments to the Social Security Act. Beginning in 1984, a portion of benefits may be taxable. How you structure your benefits can have a significant effect on the taxes you pay on your Social Security.

Before we get into the taxation of Social Security, it is important to review how your Social Security benefits are affected by the age at which you file for distributions. As the chart below shows, your benefit is reduced by 25% if you file early. PIA stands for Primary Insurance Amount which is Social Security lingo for the amount you will receive at *full retirement age* (FRA).

Apply at age	Benefit will be % of PIA	Example if PIA is $2,642
62	75.0%	$1,982
63	80.0%	$2,114
64	86.7%	$2,291
65	93.3%	$2,465

Even though you are penalized 25% if you take your benefit at 62, it is the most popular age to take benefits with over 40% of filers taking it as early as possible. This is down from over 55% who were taking benefits at 62 as recently as 2005. As the baby boomers enter retirement, they are doing more careful planning—I hope—and are making better Social Security decisions.

If you are able to delay your benefit until age 70, you will receive 132% of your full retirement benefit, as shown below.

Apply at age	Benefit will be % of PIA	Example if PIA is $2,642
66	100%	$2,642
67	108%	$2,853
68	116%	$3,064
69	124%	$3,275
70	132%	$3,486

The above chart assumes a person born between 1943 and 1954 who is entitled to the maximum Social Security benefit in 2015. Those born after 1954 have their full retirement age moved up two months for every year after 1954. For those born in 1960 and after, the full retirement age is 67.

Delaying your benefit until 70, compared to taking it at 62, more than doubles your Social Security benefit. By delaying your benefit, you are foregoing benefits for eight years; but, assuming a 2.7% *cost of living adjustment* (COLA), you will have taken more in cumulative benefits by age 79 if you delay.

If you are in poor health, or if you have no other sources of income, it may make more sense for you to take your benefits early.

We have all been told to plan for the future, not just for today. This is certainly the case with Social Security benefits. When I discuss the benefits of delaying Social Security, I put it in terms of options my clients have at different ages. Delaying benefits may require some sacrifices until age 70, such as working a few years longer or taking a part-time job. When you are relatively young, you typically have more options than you have when you are older. Most people would not want to have to get a part-time job when they are in their 80s.

The chart on the next page compares the dramatic difference in Social Security income later on in life based on filing at 62 or 70 when COLAs are factored in.

Benefit at age	If claim at 62	If claim at 70
70	$2,472	$4,347
75	$2,838	$4,991
80	$3,257	$5,729
85	$3,740	$6,576
90	$4,293	$7,550
95	$4,928	$8,667
100	$5,658	$9,950

Look at the difference in income at age 85. Again, if you have to have the income earlier or if you are in poor health, you should take your benefits early. If you can possibly delay your benefits, you should.

Taxation of Benefits

If your only source of retirement income is Social Security, the benefit is completely tax free. If you have other sources of income, some of your benefits may be included in your taxable income and taxed. Determining how much of your Social Security benefits will be taxable is a multi-step process. The amount of your benefits that is taxed depends on how much cumulative income you have, including Social Security benefits.

Provisional Income

The first step in calculating the extent of taxation on your benefits is to calculate your *provisional income*. Provisional income equals your *adjusted gross income* (AGI) plus one-half of your Social Security benefits plus tax-exempt interest. For those whose portfolio includes municipal bonds, you will undoubtedly see an issue here. While you are not taxed on the interest from these bonds, the interest received on the bonds increases your provisional income and can cause your Social Security to be taxed when it otherwise wouldn't be, thereby negating the tax advantage.

The amount of your provisional income determines the percentage of your Social Security that will be added to your other taxable income, as shown in the chart on the next page.

Filing Status	Provisional Income*	Amount of SS to Tax
Married Filing Jointly	Under $32,000	0%
	$32,000 - $44,000	up to 50%
	Over $44,000	up to 85%
Single, head of household, qualifying widow(er), maried filing separately & living apart from spouse	Under $25,000	0%
	$25,000 - $34,000	up to 50%
	Over $34,000	up to 85%
Married filing separately and living with spouse	Any amount	85%
* Provisional Income = Adjusted Gross Income + 1/2 of Social Security Benefits + Tax Exempt Interest		

Notice on this chart that if you are married filing separately and living together, 85% of your Social Security benefits will be included in taxable income, regardless of the provisional income amount. If you are using this filing status, you should review this decision with your tax advisor prior to starting your Social Security benefits.

While calculating provisional income is fairly straightforward, determining how much of your Social Security is taxed once the limits are reached is not. The IRS provides a four-page worksheet (reproduced at the end of this chapter) that you can use to manually calculate how much of your benefits will be taxed. To simplify the process, I have built a calculator to determine the percentage that will be taxed to simplify the process. Any good tax software will also calculate this for you. It is better to know ahead of time what the tax consequences are than at or after filing your return.

Percentage of Social Security Subject to Tax

Notice in the third column above it says, "up to." If your provisional income as a married filing jointly couple is over $32,000, the percentage of your Social Security that will be taxed moves up on a graduated basis, as shown in the chart on the next page.

Joint SS Benefits	AGI	Total Income	Provisional Income	Percent of Social Security Taxed
46,128	8,936	55,064	32,000	0%
46,128	13,936	60,064	37,000	5%
46,128	18,936	65,064	42,000	11%
46,128	23,936	70,064	47,000	19%
46,128	28,936	75,064	52,000	28%
46,128	33,936	80,064	57,000	37%
46,128	38,936	85,064	62,000	46%
46,128	43,936	90,064	67,000	55%
46,128	48,936	95,064	72,000	65%
46,128	53,936	100,064	77,000	74%
46,128	58,936	105,064	82,000	83%
46,128	63,936	110,064	87,000	85%

In the example above each spouse had a benefit of $1,922 per month. As you can see, it isn't until adjusted gross income (before Social Security) reaches almost $64,000 that the full 85% of benefits is taxed. When you add the joint Social Security benefits to AGI, you get total income of $110,064—so 85% of your Social Security doesn't become taxable until you have a fairly high retirement income.

In the example above, we were assuming both spouses took Social Security at age 62, which resulted in relatively low benefits. The chart below shows what happens to this couple's taxable social security calculation if they take their Social Security at age 70, which increases their joint benefit to $81,185. Note that the chart solves for the same total income as the chart above.

Joint SS Benefits	AGI	Total Income	Provisional Income	Percent of Social Security Taxed
81,185	3,879	85,064	44,472	8%
81,185	8,879	90,064	49,472	14%
81,185	13,879	95,064	54,472	18%
81,185	18,879	100,064	59,472	24%
81,185	23,879	105,064	64,472	29%
81,185	28,879	110,064	69,472	34%
81,185	33,879	115,064	74,472	39%
81,185	38,879	120,064	79,472	45%
81,185	43,879	125,064	84,472	50%
81,185	48,879	130,064	89,472	55%
81,185	53,879	135,064	94,472	60%
81,185	58,879	140,064	99,472	65%
81,185	63,879	145,064	104,472	71%
81,185	68,879	150,064	109,472	76%
81,185	73,879	155,064	114,472	81%
81,185	78,879	160,064	119,472	85%

Because only one half of your Social Security is included in provisional income, the higher the ratio of Social Security to total income, the higher your total income can be before you reach 85% taxation of your benefits.

Case Study

An example is a good way to illustrate how increasing your Social Security benefit can improve your tax position. In this example we will look at John and Mary Sample. John and Mary are both 65, each earns $60,000 per year, and each is contributing 10% towards a retirement plan. John and Mary file a joint tax return and use the standard deduction ($12,600 in 2016, $15,100 if over 65) and take their two personal exemptions ($4,050 each in 2016). Their net after-tax take home pay is $81,122 per year. They would like the same net income after they retire.

If John and Mary take their Social Security benefits at 65, they will receive total annual combined benefits of $46,128 per year. If they delay their benefits until 70, they will receive $65,229 combined per year (not adjusted for cost of living adjustments). They have sufficient investment balances to draw from in order to justify delaying their benefits. Their portfolio includes tax exempt municipal bonds which, as explained earlier, will provide very little in tax savings once they start their Social Security benefits.

If John and Mary take their benefits at age 65, 45.7% of their Social Security will be taxable. They will need to take $32,700 from their IRAs to get to their income goal. Their tax calculation is shown on the next page.

Started Social Security at 65		
Joint Social Security	46,128.00	
Excluded Social Security	(24,264.00)	
Taxable Social Security	21,864.00	47.4%
IRA Distributions	32,700.00	
Tax Exempt Interest	6,000.00	
Gross Income Subject to Tax	54,564.00	
Standard Deduction	(26,600.00)	
Personal Exemptions	-	
Federal Taxable Income	27,964.00	
Federal Income Taxes	(3,083.00)	
Net Take-home Pay	81,745.00	

In the above example, as well as throughout the rest of this book, state income taxes are not calculated. State income taxes vary considerably from state to state. Depending on the state where you live, you most likely will have to factor in state income taxes along with federal income taxes. State income taxes are typically based on federal taxable income or federal adjsuted gross income so reducing federal taxes, in most cases, also results in lowering state income tax as well. Chapter 15 outlines the major differences in taxation of retirement income for each state.

While John and Mary are not paying a huge amount of federal income taxes, the chart on the following page shows what their taxes look like at age 70 if they delay their benefits.

Started Social Security at 65		
Joint Social Security	65,230.00	
Excluded Social Security	(52,772.00)	
Taxable Social Security	12,458.00	19.1%
IRA Distributions	16,999.00	
Gross Income Subject to Tax	29,457.00	
Standard Deduction	(26,600.00)	
Personal Exemptions	-	
Federal Taxable Income	2,857.00	
Federal Income Taxes	(285.70)	
Net Take-home Pay	81,943.30	

Notice that by delaying their benefits, not only are their federal income taxes lowered significantly, they also must take much less out of their retirement plan balances. Also, notice that by delaying their Social Security until 70, they now have no tax-exempt interest. Realizing that tax-exempt interest can cause more of their Social Security to be taxed, the age 70 example liquidated their tax-exempt portfolio for living expenses until they reached age 70.

Conclusion

As we will see in coming chapters, developing a retirement income plan involves much more than analyzing your Social Security taxation and developing an estimate of your taxes in retirement. Other factors to consider are:

- The amount of your *required minimum distributions* (RMD) from retirement plans and whether these distributions will be more than needed, which could make a Roth conversion make sense
- Whether you plan to continue living in your current home
- Whether you plan to work part-time
- Investment portfolio structure to provide needed income

These factors and many others must be considered in context to put together a comprehensive retirement income plan.

IRS Worksheet 1, 2, 3, and 4 from Publication 915

While I understand most people would prefer having a root canal than to struggle through an IRS worksheet, if you are curious how much of your Social Security will be taxed, I have reproduced the IRS worksheets so your foray through this calculation might be less painful. It is usually much easier, and less prone to error, if you use a tax software program.

Bruce Larsen

Worksheet 1. Figuring Your Taxable Benefits

Keep for Your Records

Before you begin:
- If you are married filing separately and you lived apart from your spouse for all of 2015, enter "D" to the right of the word "benefits" on Form 1040, line 20a, or Form 1040A, line 14a.
- Do not use this worksheet if you repaid benefits in 2015 and your total repayments (box 4 of Forms SSA-1099 and RRB-1099) were more than your gross benefits for 2015 (box 3 of Forms SSA-1099 and RRB-1099). None of your benefits are taxable for 2015. For more information, see *Repayments More Than Gross Benefits*.
- If you are filing Form 8815, Exclusion of Interest From Series EE and I U.S. Savings Bonds Issued After 1989, do not include the amount from line 8a of Form 1040 or Form 1040A on line 3 of this worksheet. Instead, include the amount from Schedule B (Form 1040A or 1040), line 2.

1. Enter the total amount from box 5 of ALL your Forms SSA-1099 and RRB-1099. Also enter this amount on Form 1040, line 20a, or Form 1040A, line 14a	**1.** _____
2. Enter one-half of line 1	**2.** _____
3. Combine the amounts from: **Form 1040:** Lines 7, 8a, 9a, 10 through 14, 15b, 16b, 17 through 19, and 21 **Form 1040A:** Lines 7, 8a, 9a, 10, 11b, 12b, and 13	**3.** _____
4. Enter the amount, if any, from Form 1040 or 1040A, line 8b	**4.** _____
5. Enter the total of any exclusions/adjustments for: • Adoption benefits (Form 8839, line 28), • Foreign earned income or housing (Form 2555, lines 45 and 50, or Form 2555-EZ, line 18), and • Certain income of bona fide residents of American Samoa (Form 4563, line 15) or Puerto Rico	**5.** _____
6. Combine lines 2, 3, 4, and 5	**6.** _____
7. **Form 1040 filers:** Enter the amounts from Form 1040, lines 23 through 32, and any write-in adjustments you entered on the dotted line next to line 36. **Form 1040A filers:** Enter the amounts from Form 1040A, lines 16 and 17	**7.** _____
8. Is the amount on line 7 less than the amount on line 6? **No.** (stop) None of your social security benefits are taxable. Enter -0- on Form 1040, line 20b, or Form 1040A, line 14b. **Yes.** Subtract line 7 from line 6	**8.** _____
9. If you are: • Married filing jointly, enter $32,000 • Single, head of household, qualifying widow(er), or married filing separately and you lived **apart** from your spouse for all of 2015, enter $25,000 .... **Note.** If you are married filing separately and you lived with your spouse at any time in 2015, skip lines 9 through 16; multiply line 8 by 85% (0.85) and enter the result on line 17. Then go to line 18.	**9.** _____
10. Is the amount on line 9 less than the amount on line 8? **No.** (stop) None of your benefits are taxable. Enter -0- on Form 1040, line 20b, or on Form 1040A, line 14b. If you are married filing separately and you lived **apart** from your spouse for all of 2015, be sure you entered "D" to the right of the word "benefits" on Form 1040, line 20a, or on Form 1040A, line 14a. **Yes.** Subtract line 9 from line 8	**10.** _____
11. Enter $12,000 if married filing jointly; $9,000 if single, head of household, qualifying widow(er), or married filing separately and you **lived apart** from your spouse for all of 2015	**11.** _____
12. Subtract line 11 from line 10. If zero or less, enter -0-	**12.** _____
13. Enter the **smaller** of line 10 or line 11	**13.** _____
14. Enter one-half of line 13	**14.** _____
15. Enter the **smaller** of line 2 or line 14	**15.** _____
16. Multiply line 12 by 85% (0.85). If line 12 is zero, enter -0-	**16.** _____
17. Add lines 15 and 16	**17.** _____
18. Multiply line 1 by 85% (0.85)	**18.** _____
19. **Taxable benefits.** Enter the **smaller** of line 17 or line 18. Also enter this amount on Form 1040, line 20b, or Form 1040A, line 14b	**19.** _____

(TIP) *If you received a lump-sum payment in 2015 that was for an earlier year, also complete Worksheet 2 or 3 and Worksheet 4 to see if you can report a lower taxable benefit.*

**Worksheet 2. Figure Your Additional Taxable Benefits
(From a Lump-Sum Payment for a Year After 1993)**

Keep for Your Records

Enter earlier year _____

1. Enter the total amount from box 5 of ALL your Forms SSA-1099 and RRB-1099 for the earlier year, plus the lump-sum payment for the earlier year received after that year . . . . Note. If line 1 is zero or less, skip lines 2 through 20 and enter -0- on line 21. Otherwise, go on to line 2.	1. _____
2. Enter one-half of line 1	2. _____
3. Enter your adjusted gross income for the earlier year	3. _____

4. Enter the total of any exclusions/adjustments you claimed in the earlier year for:
    • Adoption benefits (Form 8839)
    • Qualified U.S. savings bond interest (Form 8815)
    • Student loan interest (Form 1040, page 1, or Form 1040A, page 1)
    • Tuition and fees (Form 1040, page 1, or Form 1040A, page 1)
    • Domestic production activities (for 2005 through 2014) (Form 1040, page 1)
    • Foreign earned income or housing (Form 2555 or Form 2555-EZ)
    • Certain income of bona fide residents of American Samoa (Form 4563) or Puerto Rico . . . .
	4. _____

5. Enter any tax-exempt interest received in the earlier year	5. _____
6. Add lines 2 through 5	6. _____
7. Enter your taxable benefits for the earlier year that you previously reported	7. _____
8. Subtract line 7 from line 6	8. _____

9. If, for the earlier year, you were:
    • Married filing jointly, enter $32,000
    • Single, head of household, qualifying widow(er), married filing separately and you lived apart from your spouse for all of the earlier year, enter $25,000 . . . .
Note. If you were married filing separately and you lived with your spouse at any time during the earlier year, skip lines 9 through 16; multiply line 8 by 85% (0.85) and enter the result on line 17. Then go to line 18.
	9. _____

10. Is the amount on line 8 more than the amount on line 9?
    No. Skip lines 10 through 20 and enter -0- on line 21.
    Yes. Subtract line 9 from line 8 . . . .
	10. _____

11. Enter $12,000 if married filing jointly for the earlier year; $9,000 if single, head of household, qualifying widow(er), or married filing separately and you **lived apart** from your spouse for all of the earlier year	11. _____
12. Subtract line 11 from line 10. If zero or less, enter -0-	12. _____
13. Enter the **smaller** of line 10 or line 11	13. _____
14. Enter one-half of line 13	14. _____
15. Enter the **smaller** of line 2 or line 14	15. _____
16. Multiply line 12 by 85% (0.85). If line 12 is zero, enter -0-	16. _____
17. Add lines 15 and 16	17. _____
18. Multiply line 1 by 85% (0.85)	18. _____
19. **Refigured taxable benefits.** Enter the **smaller** of line 17 or line 18	19. _____
20. Enter your taxable benefits for the earlier year (or as refigured due to a previous lump-sum payment for the year)	20. _____
21. **Additional taxable benefits.** Subtract line 20 from line 19. Also enter this amount on Worksheet 4, line 20	21. _____

⚠ *Do not file an amended return for this earlier year. Complete a separate Worksheet 2 or Worksheet 3 for each earlier year for which you received a lump-sum payment in 2015.*

Bruce Larsen

Worksheet 3. Figure Your Additional Taxable Benefits
(From a Lump-Sum Payment for a Year Before 1994)
Keep for Your Records

Enter earlier year ____

1.	Enter the total amount from box 5 of ALL your Forms SSA-1099 and RRB-1099 for the earlier year, plus the lump-sum payment for the earlier year received after that year .... **1.** ____	
	Note. If line 1 is zero or less, skip lines 2 through 13 and enter -0- on line 14. Otherwise, go on to line 2.	
2.	Enter one-half of line 1	**2.** ____
3.	Enter your adjusted gross income for the earlier year	**3.** ____
4.	Enter the total of any exclusions/adjustments you claimed in the earlier year for:	
	• Qualified U.S. savings bond interest (Form 8815)	
	• Foreign earned income or housing (Form 2555 or Form 2555-EZ)	
	• Certain income of bona fide residents of American Samoa (Form 4563) or Puerto Rico	**4.** ____
5.	Enter any tax-exempt interest received in the earlier year	**5.** ____
6.	Add lines 2 through 5	**6.** ____
7.	Enter your taxable benefits for the earlier year that you previously reported	**7.** ____
8.	Subtract line 7 from line 6	**8.** ____
9.	Enter $25,000 ($32,000 if married filing jointly for the earlier year; -0- if married filing separately for the earlier year and you lived with your spouse at any time during the earlier year)	**9.** ____
10.	Is the amount on line 8 more than the amount on line 9?	
	No. Skip lines 10 through 13 and enter -0- on line 14.	
	Yes. Subtract line 9 from line 8.	**10.** ____
11.	Enter one-half of line 10	**11.** ____
12.	**Refigured taxable benefits.** Enter the smaller of line 2 or line 11	**12.** ____
13.	Enter your taxable benefits for the earlier year (or as refigured due to a previous lump-sum payment for the year)	**13.** ____
14.	**Additional taxable benefits.** Subtract line 13 from line 12. Also enter this amount on Worksheet 4, line 20	**14.** ____

⚠ *Do not file an amended return for this earlier year. Complete a separate Worksheet 2 or Worksheet 3 for each earlier year for which you received a lump-sum payment in 2015.*

Publication 915 (2015)

18

A Concise Guide to Taxes in Retirement

Worksheet 4. Figure Your Taxable Benefits Under the Lump-Sum Election Method (Use With Worksheet 2 or 3)   *Keep for Your Records*

Complete Worksheet 1 and Worksheets 2 and 3 as appropriate before completing this worksheet.

1. Enter the total amount from box 5 of ALL your Forms SSA-1099 and RRB-1099 for 2015, minus the lump-sum payment for years before 2015 .... 1. _____
    Note. If line 1 is zero or less, skip lines 2 through 18, enter -0- on line 19 and go to line 20. Otherwise, go on to line 2.

2. Enter one-half of line 1 .... 2. _____

3. Enter the amount from Worksheet 1, line 3 .... 3. _____

4. Enter the amount from Worksheet 1, line 4 .... 4. _____

5. Enter the amount from Worksheet 1, line 5 .... 5. _____

6. Combine lines 2, 3, 4, and 5 .... 6. _____

7. Enter the amount from Worksheet 1, line 7 .... 7. _____

8. Subtract line 7 from line 6 .... 8. _____

9. Enter the amount from Worksheet 1, line 9. But if you are married filing separately and lived with your spouse at any time during 2015, skip lines 9 through 16; multiply line 8 by 85% (0.85) and enter the result on line 17. Then, go to line 18 .... 9. _____

10. Is the amount on line 8 more than the amount on line 9?
    No. Skip lines 10 through 18, enter -0- on line 19, and go to line 20.
    Yes. Subtract line 9 from line 8 .... 10. _____

11. Enter the amount from Worksheet 1, line 11 .... 11. _____

12. Subtract line 11 from line 10. If zero or less, enter -0- .... 12. _____

13. Enter the smaller of line 10 or line 11 .... 13. _____

14. Enter one-half of line 13 .... 14. _____

15. Enter the smaller of line 2 or line 14 .... 15. _____

16. Multiply line 12 by 85% (0.85). If line 12 is zero, enter -0- .... 16. _____

17. Add lines 15 and 16 .... 17. _____

18. Multiply line 1 by 85% (0.85) .... 18. _____

19. Enter the smaller of line 17 or line 18 .... 19. _____

20. Enter the total of the amounts from Worksheet 2, line 21, and Worksheet 3, line 14, for all earlier years for which the lump-sum payment was received .... 20. _____

21. **Taxable benefits under lump-sum election method.** Add lines 19 and 20 .... 21. _____

Next. Is line 21 above smaller than Worksheet 1, line 19?
  No. Do not use this method to figure your taxable benefits. Follow the instructions on Worksheet 1 to report your benefits.
  Yes. You can elect to report your taxable benefits under this method. **To elect this method:**

  1. Enter "LSE" to the left of Form 1040, line 20a, or Form 1040A, line 14a.

  2. If line 21 above is zero, follow the instructions in line 10 for "No" on Worksheet 1. Otherwise:

    a. Enter the amount from Worksheet 1, line 1, on Form 1040, line 20a, or on Form 1040A, line 14a.

    b. Enter the amount from line 21 above on Form 1040, line 20b, or on Form 1040A, line 14b.

    c. If you are married filing separately and you **lived apart** from your spouse for all of 2015, enter "D" to the right of the word "benefits" on Form 1040, line 20a, or Form 1040A, line 14a.

Chapter 3 – Long Term Capital Gains

Long term capital gains are generally gains taken on assets held for at least one year, with a few exceptions. Short term gains are gains realized on assets held less than one year and are generally taxed as ordinary income.

Initially, the tax rules pertaining to long term gains taken on capital assets, such as publicly traded stocks and real estate, seem fairly straightforward. Capital gains taxes are actually fairly complex and can become more so when you are in retirement. If you do a quick web search on the topic, you will get an explanation such as:

If you are in the 15% or lower bracket your capital gain tax rate is 0%; from the 25% to the 35% bracket your rate is 15%, and if you are in the 35% + bracket your rate is 20%.

If this is as far as you develop your understanding of capital gain taxes, you could be in for a big surprise if you realize a substantial capital gain in retirement. For instance, a retired couple filing a joint return with income from Social Security and IRA distributions of $72,000 is in the 10% bracket so the couple may assume they could take a $100,000 capital gain and pay no capital gain taxes. This is an incorrect assumption because brackets are determined by adjusted gross income. AGI includes capital gains; consequently, this couple's AGI will be $172,000, which moves them into the 28% bracket for determination of the top capital gain tax rate.

The tax calculation then applies ordinary income tax rates to the regular income and capital gain tax rates to the gain taken. It is possible to pay a higher effective rate on capital gains than you would pay on your ordinary income.

As an added negative consequence for the couple above, the capital gain being included in AGI can also dramatically increase the amount of their Social Security benefits that will be included in taxable income. Retirees can find themselves in a position where they are effectively double taxed on any gains they take due to the increase in Social Security subject to taxation.

Many people enter retirement owning rental real estate. They may assume that because they will be in a lower tax bracket they can sell the property and take the gains sometime during their retirement with minimal taxation. As outlined above, this is probably not the case. In addition to regular capital gain taxes, they may also have to pay 25% on the recapture of any depreciation taken or allowable. This can get really ugly. For instance, if they are in retirement and depreciating a rental property and are only in the 15% bracket, the depreciation deduction is "worth" 15% to them. As soon as they sell, they will pay a 25% rate on the recapture, more than the 15% break on taxes they received when the deduction was taken.

Before taking a substantial gain on an asset, you should ask your tax professional to calculate how the gain will affect your taxes. The calculations are very complex, especially when the alternative minimum tax is added to the mix. Rather than fight through the necessary schedules and forms, it is much easier for your tax professional to enter that transaction in his software and have the software calculate the taxes with and without the gain being taken. That being said, running through a couple of examples should give you a feel for how capital gains will affect your overall tax calculation.

Sale of a Publicly Traded Stock with a Long-Term Capital Gain

Tom and Sally Mills purchased stock in Tom's company several years ago. They are now retired and debt free. They have developed a budget of $6,000 per month spending after tax. Their retirement cash flow comes from joint Social Security benefits of $50,400 per year along with distributions from their IRAs. Their baseline tax calculation is shown on the following page.

Tom and Sally Baseline Income and Taxes	
Tom's Social Security	26,400.00
Sally's Social Security	24,000.00
Total Social Security	50,400.00
Less: Excluded Social Security	(39,980.00)
Taxable Social Security	10,420.00 21%
Tom's IRA Distributions	12,000.00
Sally's IRA Distributions	12,000.00
Adjusted Gross Income	34,420.00
Standard Deduction	(26,600.00)
Personal Exemptions	-
Taxable Income	7,820.00
Federal Taxes	(782.00)
Total Cash Flow	74,400.00
Less: Federal Taxes	(782.00)
Net After Tax Income	73,618.00

Tom and Sally are in a fairly benign tax situation. Because only 21% of their Social Security is being taxed, their taxable income is only $7,820 on $74,400 of retirement cash flow. This puts them in the 10% tax bracket.

When I prepare retirement projections, it is often helpful to look at total effective tax rate on cash flow rather than on marginal tax rates. Tom and Sally have an effective tax rate of only 1% on their total cash flow. If they were still working, and the $74,400 was W-2 income, their effective rate would be about 9.6%, and they would pay about $7,142.50 in federal taxes. Very good news for Tom and Sally's taxes in retirement.

Tom had a great deal of confidence in his company while he was on the scene. Now that he is retired and can't watch the daily operations of the company, his confidence has fallen off. After discussing the stock with Sally, they both decide they would be more comfortable selling the company stock and diversifying into several other investments.

The Mills look over their previous year's tax return and make the same assumption many people do—they are in the 10% bracket so they won't have to pay any capital gain taxes. They sell the stock.

The next year's tax return comes as an ugly shock to the tune of an additional $5,622 due in federal taxes! The chart below shows what happens to Tom and Sally if they realize the $50,000 of long term gain on his stock, assuming the stock is worth $100,000.

Tom and Sally Taxes after Taking Gain		
Tom's Social Security	26,400.00	
Sally's Social Security	24,000.00	
Total Social Security	50,400.00	
Less: Excluded Social Security	(7,560.00)	
Taxable Social Security	42,840.00	85%
Long Term Capital Gain	50,000.00	
Tom's IRA Distributions	12,000.00	
Sally's IRA Distributions	12,000.00	
Adjusted Gross Income	116,840.00	
Standard Deduction	(26,600.00)	
Personal Exemptions	-	
Taxable Income	90,240.00	
Federal Income Tax	(4,448.00)	
Capital Gain Tax	(1,956.00)	
Total Cash Flow	174,400.00	
Less: Federal Taxes	(6,404.00)	
Net After Tax Income	167,996.00	

We can see here that several undesirable things have happened to their tax status. First, the $50,000 long term capital gain has increased the percentage of Social Security subject to taxation to the maximum of 85%. So we have a bizarre situation where adding $50,000 of long term gain has increased AGI by $82,420. This also moves us up the scale to determine the capital gain tax rates that will be applied.

While it isn't technically correct from the IRS's standpoint to state it this way, the amount of tax on the capital gain is effectively 12.8% due to the coalescence of other issues when the gain is taken. Tom and Sally had the mistaken belief that, because they were in the 10% tax bracket, their capital gains tax rate would be 0%. This is a very nasty $5,622 surprise when they show up at their accountant's office to sign their return.

Is there anything Tom and Sally can have done to soften the blow? Yes— they could have spread the gain over two years. This would increase their taxes by "only" $2,325 per year ($4,650 total for the two years). This would have saved them $1,754 in taxes over the two-year period. Spreading it out over an even longer period would have increased the savings even more.

There are other more advanced strategies for controlling capital gains that can be used when selling a very large asset such as commercial real estate, a farm, or a large stock position. It may be possible to sell an asset on an installment basis that can spread the taxes over several years.

For people who are charitably inclined, it is possible to donate an asset to a charitable entity (that the donor controls) and receive a large tax deduction as well as receive a lifetime income. This type of strategy doesn't eliminate the tax entirely, but it can spread it over a very long time—even life. These types of strategies will be more fully discussed in a later chapter.

Sale of Residential Rental Real Estate

Typically, holders of residential rental real estate take a depreciation deduction each year, which lowers the taxable income attributable to the property. When the asset is sold, the IRS requires the seller to "recapture" the depreciation taken on the asset while held. Recapturing depreciation can increase the effective capital gain taxes on rental real estate. While there are plenty of advertisers telling you all the wonderful benefits of owning rental properties, very few tell you the negative tax consequences of eventually selling real estate holdings.

Capital gain taxes on rental real estate, as well as other capital assets, can be entirely eliminated; all you have to do is die! Your heirs will then be able to step-up the basis to fair market value and, if they immediately sell the asset, they will owe no taxes. This is the plan that many holders of rental properties are following, but many neglect to consider whether or not they will want to be managing the properties when they are in their 80s or 90s.

Let's go back to Tom and Sally. This time, instead of owning a stock, they own a rental property. They paid $150,000 for the property 10 years ago, and it is now worth $250,000. They are receiving rent of $1,500 per month, which gives them total annual rent of $18,000. Taxes, insurance and maintenance cost them about $5,000. Assuming they allocated 80% of the purchase price to the structure and 20% to the land the house is on, they have a depreciable basis of $120,000. Using straight line depreciation, they can take a depreciation deduction of about $4,364. This gives them cash flow of $13,000 per year and taxable income of $8,636.

Tom and Sally's long-term tenants recently moved out. Tom and Sally have spent the last two weeks getting the property ready for new tenants. They have replaced the carpets and repainted most of the rooms. They also notice that the kitchen and bathroom fixtures are getting somewhat dated and will have to be upgraded soon to continue to drive good rent.

While relaxing after a hard day, Sally says, "Tom, how much longer can we keep up this kind of work? With your bad knee and my arthritis, at some point we won't be able to do the maintenance on the place."

Tom agrees and says, "We could always hire a property manager, but then we would have to give up 8% to 10% of our income. We bought the place when Tim (their son) was in high school. Our assumption was he would help with the maintenance as we got older since he stood to inherit the property eventually. Now that he and his wife have moved out of state, that assumption is out the window."

Sally says, "Let's see if we can find a passive investment that would give us the same income."

The Mills may be moving in the right direction, but before continuing down this path, they need to see what the tax bill will look like.

They have found an investment that yields 7%, which, if they sold the house, would give them income of $17,500 per year, $4,500 more than they are getting out of the rental property.

Tom and Sally's current tax calculation is shown on the next page.

Tom and Sally Baseline Income and Taxes		
Tom's Social Security	26,400.00	
Sally's Social Security	24,000.00	
Total Social Security	50,400.00	
Less: Excluded Social Security	(39,439.00)	
Taxable Social Security	10,961.00	22%
Tom's IRA Distributions	4,000.00	
Real Estate Taxable Income	8,636.00	13,000.00 Cash Flow
Sally's IRA Distributions	12,000.00	
Adjusted Gross Income	35,597.00	
Standard Deduction	(26,600.00)	
Personal Exemptions	-	
Taxable Income	8,997.00	
Federal Taxes	(900.00)	
Total Cash Flow	79,400.00	
Less: Federal Taxes	(900.00)	
Net After Tax Income	78,500.00	

If they sell the rental property on December 31st of this year for $250,000 and invest the proceeds in the 7% investment the following year, their taxes the year of the sale is shown on the next page.

Tom and Sally Sell Rental Property		
Tom's Social Security	26,400.00	
Sally's Social Security	24,000.00	
Total Social Security	50,400.00	
Less: Excluded Social Security	(7,560.00)	
Taxable Social Security	42,840.00	85%
Tom's IRA Distributions	4,000.00	
Real Estate Taxable Income	-	
Gain on Sale	56,360.00	
Depreciation Recapture	43,640.00	
Sally's IRA Distributions	12,000.00	
Adjusted Gross Income	158,840.00	
Standard Deduction	(26,600.00)	
Personal Exemptions	-	
Taxable Income	132,240.00	
Federal Taxes	(16,981.00)	
Total Cash Flow	329,400.00	
Less: Federal Taxes	(16,981.00)	
Net After Tax Income	312,419.00	

Their net after tax cash flow on the sale is $233,919. Investing that at 7% will provide income of $16,374, which appears to make them better off. However, the increased income puts them in a different tax situation, and they also don't have the depreciation deduction. To complete the analysis, we have to see what their tax calculation is after they invest the proceeds. On the next page we can see what their financial status looks like after investing in the 7% yield investment.

Tom and Sally Income with 7% Yield Investment	
Tom's Social Security	26,400.00
Sally's Social Security	24,000.00
Total Social Security	50,400.00
Less: Excluded Social Security	(32,862.00)
Taxable Social Security	17,538.00 35%
Tom's IRA Distributions	4,000.00
Interest Income	16,374.00
Sally's IRA Distributions	12,000.00
Adjusted Gross Income	49,912.00
Standard Deduction	(26,600.00)
Personal Exemptions	-
Taxable Income	23,312.00
Federal Taxes	(2,416.00)
Total Cash Flow	82,774.00
Less: Federal Taxes	(2,416.00)
Net After Tax Income	80,358.00

Tom and Sally's before tax cash flow has increased by $3,374 annually, but their net after tax cash flow has increased by only $1,858. This is due to the interest income being taxed more than the rental cash flow because they have lost the depreciation deduction. Also, because of the increase in taxable income, more of their Social Security is also taxed.

While it doesn't appear that the couple has picked up much income, they have reduced the requirement to manage the rental real estate. Also, they will eventually lose the depreciation deduction, which would put the taxation of the property income on par with the interest income once the property is fully depreciated.

Sale of Personal Residence

A gain on the sale of a personal residence, up to $500,000 for a joint couple or $250,000 for a single filer, is **excluded** from income. The word *excluded* is important from a taxation on Social Security standpoint. If the gain were included in adjusted gross income and then deducted as an itemized deduction, more Social Security would be taxable. By its being designated excluded, it is not included in AGI and as such has no effect on the taxation of Social Security.

The exclusion is available provided the owner(s) lived in the house for 2 of the past 5 years prior to sale. A planning consideration to keep in mind is the doubling of the exclusion for joint filers compared to single filers. Often when one spouse passes away, the remaining spouse chooses to downsize. If there is over $250,000 in gain in the residence, the surviving spouse should be advised to do it before he or she is required to move to single filer status.

Conclusion

For retirees, especially those who have started their Social Security, a careful analysis should be done prior to selling a capital asset. It can often make sense, depending on the type of asset, to spread the sale over several years if possible. Due to the increased taxation of Social Security, you may want to delay taking your benefits until capital asset sales are completed. If you are already taking your benefits, and have reached full Social Security retirement age, you may want to consider suspending your benefits the year you make the sale if you are under 70.

To get a more complete understanding of how taxation of capital gains is calculated, I've included the IRS's capital gain worksheet. The helpful people at the IRS have limited this worksheet to one page, below the root canal line, so it isn't as tough to get through as the Social Security worksheets.

IRS Capital Gain Worksheet

Qualified Dividends and Capital Gain Tax Worksheet—Line 44   *Keep for Your Records*

Before you begin:	✓ See the earlier instructions for line 44 to see if you can use this worksheet to figure your tax. ✓ Before completing this worksheet, complete Form 1040 through line 43. ✓ If you do not have to file Schedule D and you received capital gain distributions, be sure you checked the box on line 13 of Form 1040.

1. Enter the amount from Form 1040, line 43. However, if you are filing Form 2555 or 2555-EZ (relating to foreign earned income), enter the amount from line 3 of the Foreign Earned Income Tax Worksheet .... **1.** _____

2. Enter the amount from Form 1040, line 9b* .... **2.** _____

3. Are you filing Schedule D?*
   ☐ **Yes.** Enter the **smaller** of line 15 or 16 of Schedule D. If either line 15 or line 16 is blank or a loss, enter -0-
   ☐ **No.** Enter the amount from Form 1040, line 13 **3.** _____

4. Add lines 2 and 3 .... **4.** _____

5. If filing Form 4952 (used to figure investment interest expense deduction), enter any amount from line 4g of that form. Otherwise, enter -0- .... **5.** _____

6. Subtract line 5 from line 4. If zero or less, enter -0- .... **6.** _____

7. Subtract line 6 from line 1. If zero or less, enter -0- .... **7.** _____

8. Enter:
   $36,250 if single or married filing separately,
   $72,500 if married filing jointly or qualifying widow(er),
   $48,600 if head of household. .... **8.** _____

9. Enter the smaller of line 1 or line 8 .... **9.** _____

10. Enter the smaller of line 7 or line 9 .... **10.** _____

11. Subtract line 10 from line 9. This amount is taxed at 0% .... **11.** _____

12. Enter the smaller of line 1 or line 6 .... **12.** _____

13. Enter the amount from line 11 .... **13.** _____

14. Subtract line 13 from line 12 .... **14.** _____

15. Enter:
    $400,000 if single,
    $225,000 if married filing separately,
    $450,000 if married filing jointly or qualifying widow(er),
    $425,000 if head of household. .... **15.** _____

16. Enter the smaller of line 1 or line 15 .... **16.** _____

17. Add lines 7 and 11 .... **17.** _____

18. Subtract line 17 from line 16. If zero or less, enter -0- .... **18.** _____

19. Enter the smaller of line 14 or line 18 .... **19.** _____

20. Multiply line 19 by 15% (.15) .... **20.** _____

21. Add lines 11 and 19 .... **21.** _____

22. Subtract line 21 from line 12 .... **22.** _____

23. Multiply line 22 by 20% (.20) .... **23.** _____

24. Figure the tax on the amount on line 7. If the amount on line 7 is less than $100,000, use the Tax Table to figure the tax. If the amount on line 7 is $100,000 or more, use the Tax Computation Worksheet .... **24.** _____

25. Add lines 20, 23, and 24 .... **25.** _____

26. Figure the tax on the amount on line 1. If the amount on line 1 is less than $100,000, use the Tax Table to figure the tax. If the amount on line 1 is $100,000 or more, use the Tax Computation Worksheet .... **26.** _____

27. **Tax on all taxable income.** Enter the **smaller** of line 25 or line 26. Also include this amount on Form 1040, line 44. If you are filing Form 2555 or 2555-EZ, do not enter this amount on Form 1040, line 44. Instead, enter it on line 4 of the Foreign Earned Income Tax Worksheet .... **27.** _____

If you are filing Form 2555 or 2555-EZ, see the footnote in the Foreign Earned Income Tax Worksheet before completing this line.

Chapter 4 – Retirement Plan Rollovers

There can be several advantages to rolling over an employer sponsored retirement account to an IRA. In this chapter we are only going to look at the tax advantages of rolling a company plan to an IRA.

Net Unrealized Appreciation - NUA

Net unrealized appreciation (NUA) refers to publicly traded company stock held in a 401(k) type plan. Often the *cost basis* (what you paid for the stock) is considerably lower than the current price of the stock. The IRS allows you to distribute the stock out of the plan and pay ordinary income taxes on only the cost basis, not the current value of the stock. If the stock is then sold, you pay long term capital gains tax on the gain of the stock. If the stock is rolled to an IRA, all distributions are taxed as ordinary income when distributions are taken.

For example, let's assume you work for XYZ. XYZ's stock is publicly traded. Twenty years ago, when the stock first became publicly traded, you purchased 200 shares for $10.00 per share. You are now retiring from XYZ, and the stock is trading at $100. If you took advantage of the NUA rules, you could instruct your 401(k) provider to distribute the stock to a brokerage account and include $2,000 as ordinary income on your tax return. If you then sell the stock for $100 per share, you would also report $18,000 of long term capital gain. Assuming you are in the 15% tax bracket, you would pay no capital gain tax on the sale of the stock if you had no other income. This is a good outcome, but much of the advantage is lost for most people if they have a very large block of company stock and choose to take it all out using NUA.

Let's look at an example with the following variables:
- John and Mary Diller are joint filers.
- They are both retiring this year at age 66.

- They have budgeted their retirement spending at $111,000 per year.
- John's annual Social Security is $25,200 if taken at 66; ($33,264 if he delays until 70).
- Mary's annual Social Security is $21,600 if taken at 66; ($28,512 if she delays until 70).
- John has a 401(k) valued at $1,800,000, which includes 25,000 shares of XYZ stock currently trading at $60.00 per share (total value $1,500,000—cost basis $125,000).
- Mary has a 401(k) valued at $400,000 with no company stock.
- John wants to diversify the entire XYZ position because it pays no dividend.

Based on what we have just learned, it would appear on the surface that John should utilize NUA to take the stock out of his 401(k) plan. The following compares the couple's (filing jointly) taxes whether doing a full NUA transaction or rolling the entire balance to an IRA and then diversifying the position.

To understand their long term annual tax liability, the first thing to consider is their on-going tax calculation once the rollover is completed. If they take their Social Security at age 66 and do no NUA transaction, their tax scenario is shown on the next page.

Started Social Security at 66	
Joint Social Security	46,800.00
Less: Excluded Social Security	(7,020.00)
Taxable Social Security	39,780.00
IRA Distributions	76,000.00
Gross Income	115,780.00
Standard Deduction	(26,600.00)
Personal Exemptions	-
Taxable Income	89,180.00
Fedral Taxes	(11,499.00) -28.91%
Net After Tax Cash Flow	111,301.00

They will be paying taxes of $11,499 on gross income of $115,780.

If they take their Social Security at 70, their tax calculation appears in the chart on the following page.

Started Social Security at 70	
Joint Social Security	61,776.00
Less: Excluded Social Security	(9,266.00)
Taxable Social Security	52,510.00
IRA Distributions	76,000.00
Gross Income	128,510.00
Standard Deduction	(26,600.00)
Personal Exemptions	-
Taxable Income	101,910.00
Fedral Taxes	(14,299.00) -27.23%
Net After Tax Cash Flow	123,477.00

Taking Social Security at 70 provides them with more income—more than they need—but also, it means they pay more in taxes. In these two examples I kept IRA distributions constant to approximate the amounts they will have to pull out of their IRAs once they reach the required minimum distribution age of 70 ½. Taking out less would result in future RMDs being larger—better to take the distributions now so we see a minimal increase in taxes at 70 ½.

Now we should look at their financial position if they do a full NUA distribution and immediately sell the stock. In this example, we will assume they are going to delay their Social Security until 70 because they will be realizing a gain of $1,250,000 as well as realizing ordinary income of $125,000 on the cost basis of the shares.

Their taxes the year of the transaction are shown on the next page.

Year of NUA Transaction		
Cost Basis of Shares	125,000.00	
Capital Gain	1,375,000.00	
Adjusted Gross Income	1,500,000.00	
Standard Deduction	(26,600.00)	
Personal Exemptions	-	
Taxable Income	1,473,400.00	
Federal Taxes	337,300.00	22.49%
Net After Tax Cash Flow	1,162,700.00	

Paying 22.5% in federal taxes on the transaction may not seem like a large amount, but when we look at the total tax bill of $337,300, it should seem obvious that they have cut deeply into their nest egg. Assuming they can get a 5% return (ordinary income) on their money moving forward, they will be faced with the following taxes the following year, assuming they turn on their Social Security at that time (age 67).

Year of After NUA Transaction		
Joint Social Security	50,544.00	
Less: Excluded Social Security	(7,582.00)	
Taxable Social Security	42,962.00	85%
Interest Income	52,585.00	
IRA Distributions	28,000.00	
Gross Income	123,547.00	
Standard Deduction	(26,600.00)	
Personal Exemptions	-	
Taxable Income	96,947.00	
Fedral Taxes	(13,207.00)	
Net After Tax Cash Flow	117,922.00	

At first glance, it would appear that John and Mary are in good shape, but when you compare their tax rates above with the rates they would be paying if they didn't do the NUA transaction, you see that they haven't really helped themselves that much. If they could get the same 5% return on their money on a tax-exempt basis, their tax status would improve. Their calculation would look like the chart below.

Year of After NUA Transaction - Tax Exempt		
Joint Social Security	50,544.00	
Less: Excluded Social Security	(7,582.00)	
Taxable Social Security	42,962.00	85%
Exempt Interest Income	52,585.00	
IRA Distributions	28,000.00	
Gross Income	70,962.00	
Standard Deduction	(26,600.00)	
Personal Exemptions	-	
Taxable Income	44,362.00	
Fedral Taxes	(4,942.00)	
Net After Tax Cash Flow	126,187.00	

This looks like a much better position for John and Mary, but this outcome assumes that they can realize a tax-exempt return of 5%, which in the current environment is only available in leveraged closed-in municipal bond funds. This scenario, because of the leverage, subjects investors to high volatility.

At this point, John and Mary's total investment balance is $1,751,700 (the remaining IRA balances of $700,000 plus after tax amount of NUA transaction less one year's living expense). Had they not done the NUA transaction, their balance would have been $2,200,000. They have reduced their total investment balance by $448,300. Over time, the balance will build back up, but if they both pass away at young ages, they will have substantially reduced the amount they can leave to their heirs.

I realize that this example is difficult to follow. The main thing to take away from this section is that while NUA seems like a good idea (a 401(k) call center employee told one of my clients it was a "no-brainer"), an in-depth tax analysis needs to be completed to see if a NUA transaction is actually to your advantage.

In my experience, it is often detrimental to do a full NUA distribution of a large block of stock. However, it often makes sense to do a partial NUA distribution, especially if the age 70 ½ RMDs will exceed what the client needs.

Age 55 Distributions

Most are aware that taking an IRA distribution before 59 ½ generally results in a 10% penalty for early withdrawal. There are some exceptions to this, such as down payment on a personal residence and taking substantial equal payments, referred to as 72(t) distributions (discussed in the next chapter). One exception that few people are aware of is the ability to take penalty-free distributions from company retirement plans at age 55 or older. The conditions to allow for these earlier distributions are:

- You must turn at least 55 the year you retire
- You must be fully retired
- You must leave funds in the company plan

While this section also belongs in the chapter on IRA distributions, it is important to consider all IRA distribution options when doing a rollover from a company plan. If you are retiring between 55 and 59 ½, you should consider leaving some funds in your company plan to cover expenses until you reach 59 ½.

Direct and Indirect Rollovers

A *direct rollover* is a transaction that has your 401(k) provider send the funds directly to an IRA you have established. Many providers actually send the rollover check to you made out to the IRA custodian for your benefit so you can't deposit it anywhere except the IRA custodian. This is by far the best way to process your rollover.

If you do an *indirect rollover*, the 401(k) provider issues the check in your name, and you have 60 days to deposit the check in an IRA account. If you miss the 60-day deadline, the IRS will consider the transaction a distribution and you will be subject to ordinary income taxes on the entire distribution.

These two methods seem very similar. As long as you get the funds deposited in 60 days, there is no difference, right? Wrong! When a 401(k) provider issues the check to you, he is required to withhold 20% of the rollover amount and forward the funds to the IRS. I guess the IRS assumes you aren't going to make the deadline, and they want to be sure they get their money.

The problem with this is that the 20% withholding is considered a distribution, despite the fact that it is being sent to the IRS, so you have to recognize the tax deposit as ordinary income unless you have money elsewhere with which you can replace the distribution taken from the IRA. This is a ridiculous place to find yourself in. It makes much more sense to establish an IRA account and do the direct rollover.

If you are not retiring, but are changing companies, the tax consequences are the same regardless of whether you are moving the funds to a new company plan or to an IRA.

You are permitted to do an indirect rollover from one IRA to another IRA, but you can do only one per year. The 20% mandatory withholding does not apply—usually—but it is a much cleaner transaction to do a tax-free custodian-to-custodian transfer. Any time IRA funds are distributed on a check made out to you there is a risk of unnecessary taxation.

You can do unlimited IRA to IRA transfers throughout the year. A rollover and a transfer sound like the same thing, but they are much different in the eyes of the IRS. To be safe, always use a custodian-to-custodian transfer rather than a rollover if you are moving funds from one IRA to another.

After Tax Funds in Company Retirement Plans

The rules around company plans have changed over the years. While you are not typically allowed to deposit after tax money in a company retirement plan (other than Roth contributions) if you were in a company plan several years ago, it is possible that you have some *after-tax* money in the plan. These are funds that found their way into the plan for which contributions you did not receive a deduction.

If you have after-tax money in your company plan and do a rollover, the after-tax money will be sent to you on a check separate from the rollover check. This money should be deposited into a Roth IRA account so that all earnings are tax-free rather than deposited into a brokerage or saving account, which would then subject all earnings to taxes.

Direct Rollover of Traditional 401(k) Funds to Roth 401(k)

This is very simple—don't do it. If you rollover your traditional 401(k) funds to a Roth 401(k), you will pay ordinary income taxes on the amount of the rollover. While there may be very good reasons to convert some traditional 401(k) funds to a Roth, doing it directly eliminates your ability to change your mind and later re-characterize your Roth 401(k) back to a traditional 401(k) (more fully explored in the chapter on Roth conversions). A better method is to roll the funds to a traditional IRA, then convert that IRA to a Roth.

The new tax code, as of 2018, also eliminated the ability to recharacterize Roth IRA conversions, but as this provision sunsets in 2025 the advantage to doing conversion outside of 401(k)'s may return.

Conclusion

There are entire books devoted to managing IRAs. What I have attempted to do here is point out several tax traps when rolling a company plan. For many retirees the rollover transaction is perhaps the single largest financial transaction of their lives. It should go without saying that competent advice should be sought before entering into the transaction.

For a complete understanding of the tax consequences of IRA rollovers, as well as the topic of the next chapter—IRA distributions—see IRS Publications 590-B. In case you're wondering, Publication 590-A covers contributions to IRAs. Readers close to or in retirement probably have figured this out already.

Chapter 5 – IRA Distributions

When we contribute to IRAs or company retirement plans, we basically make a deal with the IRS. We agree that in exchange for a deduction from taxable income the year of the contributions we will pay taxes later when we take the money out. This seems like a good deal because it is assumed we will be in a lower tax bracket when we retire than we are when we are working. While this may be true for most people, most of the people I have worked with over the years want the same in net after-tax cash flow in retirement that they had while working.

Even if you are in a lower tax bracket in retirement than you were while working, the amount of tax you pay could well be much higher than the savings you realized when you took the deduction on the contribution. For example, let's assume you made a deductible contribution of $2,000 to an IRA 20 years ago when you were in the 25% federal tax bracket. The deduction at that time saved you $500 in taxes. Assuming a 6% rate of return, the $2,000 would have grown to $6,414.27. You now decide to distribute the entire amount out. Assuming you are now in a lower bracket of 15%, your tax bill on the distribution would be $962.14. While it is nice that your $2,000 contribution, that only cost you $1,500 because of the tax savings, grew to a net after-tax distribution of $5,452,13, it was also a pretty good deal for the IRS. Their "investment" of $500 in tax savings 20 years ago grew to $962.14.

If a Roth account would have been available, you could have contributed $1,500 (the net of what a deductible IRA contribution cost you), and it would have grown to $4,810 in 20 years at the same 6% growth rate. So if your assumption that you will be in a lower tax bracket is valid, the traditional IRA was a better deal for you, even though you paid more taxes on the distribution than you saved when you made the contribution.

As we saw previously, things aren't quite that simple when we factor in Social Security. Remember that taxation of Social Security depends on the amount of cumulative total income. Let's carry the $6,414.27 distribution of our hypothetical example all the way through a client's tax return. Let's assume they are joint filers and each is receiving $24,000 per year in Social Security and they also have $50,000 in other ordinary income—such as pension or interest income. For this couple 66% of their Social Security income is taxable, and they are in the 15% bracket. Their total federal tax bill is $8,207.50. Knowing that they are in the 15% bracket, we would expect the $6,414.27 distribution to cost them $962.14 in additional taxes. Adding the additional $6,414.27 to their AGI now causes 77% of their Social Security to be taxable, which causes their total federal taxes to go up to $9,987.46. Their all-in tax bill on the distribution is actually $1,779.96, not the $962.14 that was expected. That makes the effective tax rate 27.75% when 15% was expected! The couple's net after tax distribution of $4,634.31 makes the Roth option distribution of $4,810 look more appealing.

For those people who are facing having 85% of their Social Security being taxed, regardless of IRA distributions, this issue disappears. But for most people who are looking at retirement income between $60,000 and $160,000 annually after tax, the "double taxation" that results as more ordinary income is added is considerable.

It is my opinion that saving via a Roth IRA is a much better decision for most middle-income people. While that deduction going into a traditional account is appealing, I like the certainty (as much as anything can be certain) of knowing Roth distributions will have no tax liability and cause no more of my Social Security to be taxed. When we look at historical tax rates, and put that up against the huge national debt, an argument can be made that tax rates are certain to rise, despite coming down with the 2018 tax act.

Section 72(t) Early Distributions

As most know, taking distributions out of an IRA before 59 ½ can subject you to a 10% penalty on the amount withdrawn. However, you are actually able to take penalty free withdrawals from an IRA at any age, provided the withdrawals are substantial and equal and will continue for at least 5 years, or until you reach age 59 ½, whichever is the longer time frame.

The IRS allows you to use three calculation methods: amortization, minimum distribution, and annuity to calculate the allowed 72(t) distribution amount. Each of these methods uses a standard interest rate that is not more than 120% of the federal mid-term rate for either of the two months immediately preceding the month in which the distribution begins. The *Applicable Federal*

Rates (AFR) are published monthly by the U.S. Treasury on or about the 22nd of each month.

I realize that for many the above declaration may read like a foreign language, as many federal regulations do. Fortunately, you do not need to do the math to calculate how much you can take out of an IRA if you are under age 59 ½. There are several accurate calculators on the internet that can do this for you. An internet search for "72(t) calculator" will bring the calculators up.

Using an example should help explain the calculation. John Smith was born 6/23/1963 and is currently 54 years old. John was a very good saver in his company retirement plan, and the plan also had a very generous match. His current balance is $2,000,000. John has read that taking a 4% distribution from a retirement plan should be sustainable for life without running out of money. Four percent of the $2,000,000 balance is $80,000, which John feels is plenty to provide for his retirement needs since he is completely debt free.

John wants to know if he can use 72(t) to take distributions from his rollover until he is 59 ½. Finding an online calculator, John enters his information as follows:

John Smith - 72(t) Calculations	
Date of Birth	6/23/1963
IRA Balance	2,000,000.00
First Payment Date	8/2/2018
120% of Mid-term Rate	1.71%
Expected Investment Return	6.00%

Some calculators will ask for additional inputs that can be changed to increase or decrease the results slightly. The results of these variables being entered display the maximum amount John can withdraw penalty free as shown on the next page.

John Smith - Maximum 72t Withdrawals	
Method	
Minimum Distribution	46,948.36
Amortization	66,489.51
Annuity	65,494.32

The most John can distribute penalty free is $66,489.51, a figure less than the $80,000 he needs. The low distribution is caused by the historically low mid-term rate. If the rate were higher, John's distributions would also be higher.

John may make the incorrect assumption that he could take out the $66,489.51 each year penalty free and take out the balance of $13,510.49 and pay the 10% penalty on only the excess distribution. The rules on 72(t) distributions are very strict and say that if distributions exceed the maximum allowed, all distributions will be subject to the 10% early withdrawal penalty. Other important rules state that money cannot be added to the IRA, and the distributions must continue for the longer of 5 years or until age 59 ½.

So, does John have any other options? Yes, he does. The rules around 72(t) distributions apply only to a specific IRA account. John could move $120,000 to a separate IRA and calculate his 72(t) distribution on the remaining $1,880,000. The 72(t) maximum distribution would be $62,500.14. Out of the other IRA he could withdraw the balance of $19,250 to cover the remainder desired and to pay the 10% penalty on the smaller distribution. Keep in mind that the entire distribution is taxed as ordinary income, so John should then calculate his net after-tax/after-penalty income to make sure it will cover his needs.

Another option for John would be to continue working until January of the following year before retiring. John could then leave money in his 401(k), which as mentioned in the previous chapter, can be withdrawn penalty free as long as John reaches age 55 the year he retires and is indeed fully retired.

Required Minimum Distributions (RMDs)

Most people are aware that in the year they turn 70 ½ they have to start taking required minimum distributions from their IRAs or 401(k)s. The amount of the RMD increases each year as shown on the table below.

Required Minimum Distributions					
Age	Factor	%	Age	Factor	%
70	27.4	3.65%	93	9.6	10.42%
71	26.5	3.77%	94	9.1	10.99%
72	25.6	3.91%	95	8.6	11.63%
73	24.7	4.05%	96	8.1	12.35%
74	23.8	4.20%	97	7.6	13.16%
75	22.9	4.37%	98	7.1	14.08%
76	22.0	4.55%	99	6.7	14.93%
77	21.2	4.72%	100	6.3	15.87%
78	20.3	4.93%	101	5.9	16.95%
79	19.5	5.13%	102	5.5	18.18%
80	18.7	5.35%	103	5.2	19.23%
81	17.9	5.59%	104	4.9	20.41%
82	17.1	5.85%	105	4.5	22.22%
83	16.3	6.13%	106	4.2	23.81%
84	15.5	6.45%	107	3.9	25.64%
85	14.8	6.76%	108	3.7	27.03%
86	14.1	7.09%	109	3.4	29.41%
87	13.4	7.46%	110	3.1	32.26%
88	12.7	7.87%	111	2.9	34.48%
89	12.0	8.33%	112	2.6	38.46%
90	11.4	8.77%	113	2.4	41.67%
91	10.8	9.26%	114	2.1	47.62%
92	10.2	9.80%	115+	1.9	52.63%

As we can see, the distribution percentage increases each year. Anyone living beyond normal life expectancy will come very close to depleting their IRA unless they are getting a huge rate of return. As the distribution amount moves up, so does the tax bill. Refusing to take an RMD isn't an option. The penalty is 50% of the amount that should have been withdrawn.

The table above is the *Uniform Life Table*. If you have a spouse that is more than 10 years younger than you, you should use the *Joint Life and Last Survivor Expectancy Table*. This table uses both your age and your spouse's age to calculate the RMD, which results in lower distribution requirements.

Having an increasing amount being distributed over your lifetime isn't necessarily a bad thing. After all, we know inflation is almost as certain as death and taxes, so we would expect to need more over time. Taking larger distributions to keep pace with inflation is partially mitigated by the tax bracket's being indexed to the *Chained Consumer Price Index* (Chained-CPI) each year. The problem for most tax payers is that the limits set for taxability of Social Security are not indexed for inflation. As Social Security payments are not indexed for inflation each year, more and more people will find themselves paying more and more tax on their Social Security.

Let's look at a middle of the road retirement example. Dan and Mary Dugan are joint filers who will be 70 ½ this year. Their joint Social Security benefits are $48,000, and Mary has a $600,000 IRA with a projected 6% annual return. The Social Security and RMD will provide Mary and Dan with a little over $69,000 in after tax income this year. Their effective tax rate on income is 3.9%.

If we use the long-term average CPI rate of 2.6% and apply it to their Social Security cost of living adjustment and we apply the Chained-CPI to the standard deduction and personal exemptions, we can see on the next page that their taxable income goes up each year. Even with the increases in Social Security and an increased RMD, Bill and Sally will see their inflation adjusted income fall each year as their taxable income increases—even with indexed tax rates. Because the 2018 tax changes sunset in 2025 (most of them), we return to regular CPA in 2026; just to make tax planning even more complex.

Taxation of Social Security					
Age	Joint Social Security Benefits	RMD	% of Social Security Taxed	Indexed Stand Ded & Exempt	Taxable Income	Increase in Taxable Inc.
70	48,000	21,898	15.9%	26,600	2,911	
71	49,248	23,400	19.1%	27,200	5,620	93.1%
72	50,528	25,004	22.4%	27,900	8,432	50.0%
73	51,842	26,717	25.7%	28,600	11,459	35.9%
74	53,190	28,546	29.1%	29,200	14,816	29.3%
75	54,572	30,498	32.5%	30,100	18,114	22.3%
76	55,990	32,581	35.9%	30,800	21,871	20.7%
77	57,446	34,641	39.1%	31,700	25,400	16.1%
78	58,940	37,003	42.6%	29,200	32,906	29.6%
79	60,472	39,319	45.8%	29,900	37,141	12.9%
80	62,044	41,769	49.1%	30,800	41,442	11.6%
81	63,658	44,357	52.4%	31,600	46,115	11.3%
82	65,314	47,088	55.7%	32,500	50,972	10.5%
83	67,012	49,969	59.0%	33,300	56,223	10.3%
84	68,754	53,002	62.4%	34,200	61,675	9.7%
85	70,542	55,813	65.2%	35,100	66,734	8.2%
86	72,376	58,727	68.1%	36,000	72,005	7.9%
87	74,258	61,738	70.9%	36,900	77,475	7.6%
88	76,188	64,839	73.6%	37,900	83,033	7.2%
89	78,168	68,022	76.3%	38,800	88,862	7.0%
90	80,200	70,647	78.2%	39,900	93,482	5.2%
91	82,286	73,250	80.0%	40,900	98,185	5.0%
92	84,426	75,807	81.6%	41,900	102,824	4.7%

The bottom line of all this is that, to the extent possible, you should attempt to minimize your IRA distributions, either through Roth conversions or by spending the money down while delaying Social Security. We will explore this further in the chapter on Roth conversions.

Tax Withholding

When you begin taking distributions from traditional IRAs, you should try to have the federal and state taxes due on these distributions withheld as accurately as possible. If you withhold too much in taxes, your distributions will be more than they should be, which will result in more taxes. If you don't withhold enough, you may have to take an additional distribution to pay taxes when you file your return, which could place you in a higher tax bracket for the year the taxes are paid. Your tax preparer should be able to give you an accurate projection of your taxes due on distributions.

Unfortunately, most IRA custodians do not make it as easy as it should be to have accurate taxes withheld. Some custodians will only withhold your federal taxes, but not state. Many custodians set the minimum federal withholding at 10%, which is too high for many middle-income filers.

These shortcomings can be worked around. For instance, if your effective federal tax on retirement cash flow is 5%, you could withhold federal taxes for half of the year; then stop withholding the final six months of the year.

If you itemize your deductions, you can only deduct state income taxes in the year paid. If your custodian doesn't allow you to withhold state income taxes, you may want to make a deposit for the estimated state taxes before the end of the year to take the deduction. Your State and Local Taxes deduction is now capped at $10,000 per year.

Roth IRA Distributions

While it is generally the case that Roth IRA distributions are tax free, there are a few exceptions to the general rule. Contributions to Roth accounts can always be withdrawn tax free. Earnings can be withdrawn tax free as long as you have reached age 59 ½ and you have had a Roth account established for at least 5 years. The IRS assumes that contributions come out first, so as long as you withdraw less than 20% of contributions each year you will meet the 5-year holding period before earnings come out. If earnings are withdrawn before the 5-year holding period is reached, you will have to pay taxes on the earnings, but there is no penalty if you are over 59 ½.

Contributions can also be withdrawn tax and penalty free if you are under 59 ½. If earnings are withdrawn prior to reaching age 59 ½, you will be assessed a 10% early withdrawal penalty as well as being required to pay taxes on the withdrawn earnings.

The five-year holding period for contributions allows you to aggregate all Roth IRAs and use the starting date of the oldest account. If you do a traditional IRA to Roth conversion, the five-year holding period is applied to each conversion separately. Each conversion amount has its own five-year holding requirement to take out tax-free withdrawals of earnings.

Unlike traditional IRAs, Roth IRAs have no required minimum distribution for the account holder or a spousal beneficiary. For this reason, Roth accounts can provide a lot of cash flow flexibility in a retirement plan.

Inherited IRAs

As the generation that was first able to make IRA contributions is reaching normal life expectancy, more and more people have begun to inherit IRA accounts. I see more errors made with inherited IRAs than with any other tax-deferred account.

The most common error is assuming that since the beneficiary is under age 70 ½, there is no distribution requirement. This is not the case. Anyone who inherits an IRA must begin required minimum distributions the year following the benefactor's death. The amount of the distribution is based on the beneficiary's life expectancy using the IRS's Single Life Expectancy table, reproduced on the following page:

Single Life Table for Beneficiaries					
Age	Factor	%	Age	Factor	%
56	28.7	3.48%	84	8.1	12.35%
57	27.9	3.58%	85	7.6	13.16%
58	27.0	3.70%	86	7.1	14.08%
59	26.1	3.83%	87	6.7	14.93%
60	25.2	3.97%	88	6.3	15.87%
61	24.4	4.10%	89	5.9	16.95%
62	23.5	4.26%	90	5.5	18.18%
63	22.7	4.41%	91	5.2	19.23%
64	21.8	4.59%	92	4.9	20.41%
65	21.0	4.76%	93	4.6	21.74%
66	20.2	4.95%	94	4.3	23.26%
67	19.4	5.15%	95	4.1	24.39%
68	18.6	5.38%	96	3.8	26.32%
69	17.8	5.62%	97	3.6	27.78%
70	17.0	5.88%	98	3.4	29.41%
71	16.3	6.13%	99	3.1	32.26%
72	15.5	6.45%	100	2.9	34.48%
73	14.8	6.76%	101	2.7	37.04%
74	14.1	7.09%	102	2.5	40.00%
75	13.4	7.46%	103	2.3	43.48%
76	12.7	7.87%	104	2.1	47.62%
77	12.1	8.26%	105	1.9	52.63%
78	11.4	8.77%	106	1.7	58.82%
79	10.8	9.26%	107	1.5	66.67%
80	10.2	9.80%	108	1.4	71.43%
81	9.7	10.31%	109	1.2	83.33%
82	9.1	10.99%	110	1.1	90.91%
83	8.6	11.63%	111+	1.0	100.00%

The calculation to determine the RMD on an inherited IRA not only uses a different table, but a different calculation method. The year following the death of the deceased account holder, the owner of the new inherited IRA needs to look up his or her age as of the end of the current year to determine the factor to use for the first year's RMD. Unlike your own IRA, calculating the RMD on an inherited IRA does not require a return to the table each subsequent year. Instead, each year following the first year, you simply subtract 1 from the initial-year factor. While the RMD rules around your own IRA make it almost impossible to fully distribute your own IRA if you don't take out more than the minimum, an inherited IRA will most likely be fully distributed during the inherited owner's lifetime, assuming normal life expectancy. An inherited IRA owner can distribute more than the RMD, even the entire balance, with no penalties.

From a tax perspective, distributions from inherited IRAs are taxed no differently than your own IRA, but it is important to understand how they work so that errors are not made resulting in large tax penalties.

Another error I see is beneficiaries requesting distributions from the deceased IRA that they assume they can then deposit in an inherited IRA account. The IRS does not allow this unless the check is made out to the custodian of the IRA for your benefit. You should do an indirect transfer of the funds to the inherited IRA or a direct rollover. If the distribution check is made out directly to you, it is considered a distribution and cannot be deposited in an inherited IRA to preserve tax deferral.

Spousal Beneficiary

If a deceased IRA owner's beneficiary is the owner's spouse, the beneficiary spouse has two options. He or she can establish an inherited IRA or roll over the IRA into his or her own IRA. For a spouse who is under 59 ½, it typically makes sense to establish an inherited IRA. This is because there are no early withdrawal penalties for inherited IRAs. If the spouse is over 59 ½, the deceased spouse's IRA most likely should be rolled to the surviving spouse's IRA to allow for more lenient RMD rules, assuming the surviving spouse is younger than the deceased. A spousal inherited IRA can always, at a later date, be rolled to an IRA, but once rolled to the surviving spouse's IRA, it cannot be converted back to an inherited IRA.

Planning Strategies for Inherited IRAs

The age range that most children inherit IRAs from their parents is typically between 50 and 60. This also typically corresponds to the children's maximum earning years. This phenomenon presents a conundrum. Children receive a sizable taxable asset when they are in their highest lifetime tax bracket. It can often make very good tax sense for parents to convert their IRAs to Roth accounts and have the children pay the taxes on those. This will allow the children to inherit a tax-free account.

Let's look at an example how conversion could be beneficial. Mary is single and earning $195,000 per year. Her mother, Beth, is 80 and in poor health and, unfortunately, is not expected to live to the end of the year. Beth has a small pension of $15,000 per year, Social Security of $24,000 per year and an IRA valued at $374,000 that generated a current-year RMD of $20,000. Beth is paying federal taxes of $5,896.24. Mary, the daughter, is paying federal taxes of $39,278.75, after $19,500 in 401(k) contributions are accounted for. Mary has a very large 401(k) balance and realizes that when she inherits Beth's IRA, she will have large RMDs required from the inherited IRA that will result in higher taxes for the rest of her life. Mary also has a large savings account.

Once Mary inherits Beth's IRA, her taxable income will increase by $13,031, resulting in her federal tax liability moving up to $42,927.43—an increase of $3,648.68. If Beth were to convert the IRA to a Roth, there would be additional taxes due of $116,217.54. Mary could gift the money to Beth to pay the taxes, and as a consequence, Mary would inherit a tax-free account (She would still have to take out RMDs, but the distributions would be tax free.). If Mary had her own IRA with the same balance then converts to a Roth, her tax increase would be $130,394.63. While an initial savings of $14,177.09 seems small, when the tax savings over Mary's life is added in, it can be substantial.

Several years ago, three clients of mine (brothers) were anticipating inheriting their mother's IRA at some point. The mother had a pension, which along with Social Security, provided her all the money she needed. Everyone in the family realized that when her RMD was going to start, she would be paying taxes on money she didn't need. We factored in the tax savings to her by converting her entire $300,000 IRA to a Roth. The three brothers gifted her the balance needed to pay the conversion taxes. Ten years have passed (She is still in great shape.), and the account has grown to nearly $600,000, and nobody in the family will ever have to pay taxes on future distributions.

Conclusion

Along with Social Security, your largest income stream in retirement will most likely be IRA distributions. It is critically important to project what these distributions will look like so that you are not surprised by unexpected taxes or, even worse, penalties.

The baby boomers will inherit billions of dollars in taxable IRA accounts over the next several years. Part of the estate planning discussion should include the multigenerational issues of their tax-deferred accounts.

Chapter 6 – Roth Conversions

Deciding whether to convert a traditional IRA or 401(k) to a Roth can be thorny. Future tax rates are uncertain as, of course, is life expectancy. Even if we assume normal life expectancy and constant tax rates (with tax brackets indexed for inflation), the decision process is often confounded by faulty assessment of the character of the income streams being analyzed. Most calculators that I have reviewed take several short-cuts that result in inaccurate results. An accurate picture of the outcome of a Roth conversion comes into view only after a lot of hard work.

Before we get into whether a Roth conversion may make sense, let's first get an understanding of why you may want to consider a Roth conversion. There are two reasons to consider converting to a Roth: to save taxes over your lifetime or to increase your estate value (what you will leave to your kids or grandkids). The first reason (saving taxes), in my opinion, is not what you should be looking at; it isn't what you pay, but what you keep! In other words, if I pay more in taxes over my retirement years, but I have more left over at the end of my life, how much I paid in taxes really doesn't matter. Specifically, if I am paying higher taxes with a Roth conversion, but my total account balances are higher at the end of my life—it would make sense to do a Roth conversion.

Shortfalls of Roth Conversion Calculators

The typical *Roth conversion calculator* that can be found online looks like the following:

Roth Conversion Calulator	
1 Traditional IRA Balances	500,000
2 Amount you would like to convert	100,000
3 Filing Status	Joint
4 Estimated Taxable Income	82,000
5 Estimated Federal Income Tax Rate	15.00%
6 Estimated State Income Tax Rate	5.00%
7 Est. State Income Tax Rate at Withdrawal	5.00%
8 Number of Years Before Roth Withdrawal	50

Let's look at these inputs one by one.

1. **Traditional IRA Balances:** This is the easy one. It is somewhat incomplete, however, because it doesn't ask you to separate balances by spouses. Spouses with different ages will have different required minimum distribution requirements.

2. **Amount you would like to convert:** How the heck do I know; isn't your calculator supposed to help me with this?

3. **Filings Status:** Another one that seems easy, provided both spouses die the same year. If one spouse passes away earlier, the remaining spouse will have to file as a single tax payer, increasing taxes if the income is relatively constant.

4. **Estimated Taxable Income:** You don't know what this will be until you do an entire lifetime retirement budget. As you have learned in earlier chapters, your taxable income will depend on how you arrange your retirement cash flows.

5. **Estimated Federal Income Tax Rate:** Unless you have figured out Number 4, you have no clue what your estimated federal income tax rate is.

6. **Estimated State Income Tax Rate:** This rate also depends on the characterization of the income since many states exclude social security and/or pension income.

7. **Estimated State Income Tax at Withdrawal:** Who knows?

8. **Number of Years before Roth Withdrawal:** This is used to calculate how much is in the Roth net of taxes at the end of this period.

All this calculator is really doing is assuming you convert to a Roth and pay the taxes out of the IRA. Then it simply calculates how much the Roth will be worth at the end of the period (The net amount after taxes is assumed to be deposited into the Roth.).

This is a very incomplete analysis because it doesn't address the reasons for doing a Roth in the first place. To decide if a Roth conversion makes sense, you need to analyze your entire retirement financial picture. Based on experience, I'll give you a heads-up: most times conversion makes sense if your required minimum distributions exceed the amount you need, and you have sufficient savings outside the IRA to pay the taxes.

Steps to Analyze a Roth Conversion

The first step is to do a projection of your lifetime cash flow needs. Let's take a look at Bill and Susan. In order to perform this projection, the following variables will be used.

- Bill's age is 68; Susan is 67. They are retiring this year.
- Bill's life expectancy is 85; Susan's is 92.
- IRA balances of $500,000
- Savings and CDs of $100,000
- Bill's Social Security at 70 is $35,243.
- Susan's Social Security at 70 is $29,012.
- Susan has a pension of $12,000 at 67.
- Expected Social Security COLAs are 2.6%.
- Retirement cash flow needed for basic living expenses is $60,000 per year.
- Bill and Susan have calculated their healthcare expenses (including Medicare and supplemental insurance premiums) to be $4,320 per person per year, increasing 5% annually.
- Bill and Susan have 6 years remaining on their mortgage; principle and interest payments are $13,500 per year.
- Expected rate of return on IRA investments is 6.5%, 1.5% on CD's.
- Inflation is projected at 2.6%.
- They assume if one of them passes away early, the remaining spouse will need about 80% of basic living expenses.

Step 1 – Calculate Net Cash Flow Needed

Using the variables above, we can calculate Bill and Susan's inflation adjusted retirement cash flow need, tabulated on the next page.

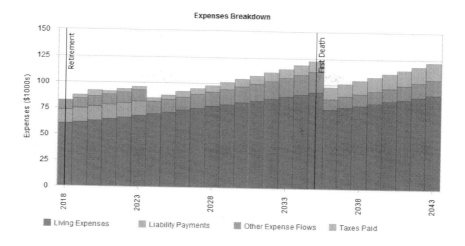

It is not uncommon to see "lumpy" cash flow needs in retirement. The first drop off in the graph is when the mortgage is paid off. The second drop off is when Bill passes away at 85. I often see other expenses early in retirement as many people have a bucket list they would like to work on while they are still young enough to enjoy themselves.

Step 2 – Determine Their Current Tax Status with no Roth Conversion

The next step in the process is to determine what the clients' tax projection looks like if they use the advice outlined earlier in this book to reduce their taxes as much as possible by making tax-smart Social Security decisions. For the example on the next page, I am using Colorado state income tax rates to have a more complete tax picture.

Year	Age	Income Flows	IRA RMD's	Total Inflows	Total Expenses	Total Outflows	Net Cash Flow	Taxes Paid	Total Portfolio Assets
2018	68/67	$12,000	$0	$12,000	$82,140	$82,140	(70,140)	$0	$563,860
2019	69/68	12,000	0	12,000	87,600	87,600	(75,600)	3,468	523,343
2020	70/69	49,099	18,987	68,086	92,077	92,077	(23,991)	5,890	514,180
2021	71/70	81,398	19,403	100,801	91,205	91,205	9,596	2,900	537,795
2022	72/71	83,203	20,633	103,836	93,672	93,672	10,164	3,182	561,659
2023	73/72	85,054	21,939	106,993	96,166	96,166	10,827	3,447	585,770
2024	74/73	86,954	23,327	110,281	85,328	85,328	24,953	3,757	623,483
2025	75/74	88,903	24,801	113,704	88,036	88,036	25,668	4,065	661,266
2026	76/75	90,903	26,366	117,269	91,865	91,865	25,404	5,419	698,008
2027	77/76	92,954	27,896	120,850	94,840	94,840	26,010	5,840	734,563
2028	78/77	95,058	29,652	124,710	97,931	97,931	26,779	6,296	770,816
2029	79/78	97,217	31,355	128,572	101,110	101,110	27,462	6,754	806,665
2030	80/79	99,432	33,144	132,576	104,389	104,389	28,187	7,224	841,995
2031	81/80	101,705	35,025	136,730	107,800	107,800	28,930	7,736	876,651
2032	82/81	104,037	36,998	141,035	111,320	111,320	29,715	8,264	910,492
2033	83/82	106,430	39,067	145,497	114,966	114,966	30,531	8,819	943,348
2034	84/83	108,886	41,234	150,120	118,745	118,745	31,375	9,407	975,032
2035	85/84	111,405	43,205	154,610	122,576	122,576	32,034	9,942	1,005,424
2036	86/85	67,940	43,094	111,034	97,780	97,780	13,254	11,192	1,017,040
2037	87/86	69,395	45,117	114,512	101,066	101,066	13,446	11,977	1,026,719
2038	88/87	70,888	47,193	118,081	104,408	104,408	13,673	12,741	1,034,304
2039	89/88	72,419	49,315	121,734	107,881	107,881	13,853	13,556	1,039,551
2040	90/89	73,990	51,474	125,464	111,433	111,433	14,031	14,367	1,042,258
2041	91/90	75,602	53,190	128,792	114,874	114,874	13,918	14,981	1,042,400
2042	92/91	77,256	54,869	132,125	118,365	118,365	13,760	15,556	1,039,809
2043	93/92	78,952	56,494	135,446	121,934	121,934	13,512	16,117	1,034,283

Notice that Bill and Susan recognize they will have RMDs higher than they need once Social Security is started, based on the positive cash flow in the Net Cash Flow column. In 2032, one year after Bill has passed away, Susan will have to file as a single taxpayer, rather than joint. This will cause taxes to go up, even though her expenses are less than their prior joint need (80% of basic living expenses and only one health care expense).

The most complicated calculation in the above spreadsheet is the "Total Taxes" column. Some tax software doesn't allow for indexing of tax brackets. Each year, the IRS moves the brackets up in line with inflation. If you adjust everything else, but leave the brackets constant, you end up with much higher taxes later in life. This issue is complicated further by the change in tax law for 2018 and the sunsetting of these changes in 2025.

When Susan is 92, her investments total $1,034,283. This figure comprises a cash savings balance of $447,082 and an IRA balance of $557,201. Susan and Bill paid total taxes of $212,897 over their retirement years. This is a very nice outcome; they got themselves through a long retirement without depleting their assets. They now want to know if they can do even better by converting some of their IRA money to a Roth.

Step 3 – Determine if a Roth Conversion Improves Their Position

Seeing that their required minimum distributions are going to exceed what they need, Bill and Susan make the assumption that their IRA balances are "too big." They want to see what things look like if they do a full or partial Roth conversion, realizing that the amount of the conversion is taxed just like an IRA distribution.

They first see what happens if they convert it all. It becomes clear right away that converting it all may not a good idea. Taxes due in the year of the conversion are $33,226. This is more than they have in their savings so they would have to pull money out of the converted Roth to pay taxes, which defeats the purpose. They decide to convert half of the IRA and spread it over two years. Their long-term projection is shown below.

Year	Age	Income Flows	IRA RMD's	Total Inflows	Total Expenses	Total Outflows	Net Cash Flow	Taxes Paid	Total Portfolio Assets
2018	68/67	$12,000	$0	$12,000	$98,637	$98,637	($86,637)	$16,497	$547,363
2019	69/68	12,000	0	12,000	122,275	122,275	-110,275	38,143	471,924
2020	70/69	49,099	7,711	56,810	92,242	92,242	-35,432	6,055	459,292
2021	71/70	81,398	6,958	88,356	88,854	88,854	-498	549	481,690
2022	72/71	83,203	7,380	90,583	91,145	91,145	-562	655	505,058
2023	73/72	85,054	7,824	92,878	93,446	93,446	-568	727	529,495
2024	74/73	86,954	8,295	95,249	82,291	82,291	12,958	720	568,575
2025	75/74	88,903	8,819	97,722	84,781	84,781	12,941	810	608,812
2026	76/75	90,903	9,376	100,279	87,694	87,694	12,585	1,248	649,911
2027	77/76	92,954	9,920	102,874	90,366	90,366	12,508	1,366	692,242
2028	78/77	95,058	10,545	105,603	93,116	93,116	12,487	1,481	735,866
2029	79/78	97,217	11,150	108,367	95,961	95,961	12,406	1,605	780,828
2030	80/79	99,432	11,786	111,218	98,891	98,891	12,327	1,726	827,190
2031	81/80	101,705	12,455	114,160	101,931	101,931	12,229	1,867	874,998
2032	82/81	104,037	13,157	117,194	105,062	105,062	12,132	2,006	924,319
2033	83/82	106,430	13,893	120,323	108,301	108,301	12,022	2,154	975,211
2034	84/83	108,886	14,663	123,549	111,648	111,648	11,901	2,310	1,027,739
2035	85/84	111,405	15,364	126,769	115,091	115,091	11,678	2,457	1,081,984
2036	86/85	67,940	15,325	83,265	88,974	88,974	-5,709	2,386	1,121,647
2037	87/86	69,395	16,044	85,439	91,672	91,672	-6,233	2,583	1,163,017
2038	88/87	70,888	16,782	87,670	94,425	94,425	-6,755	2,758	1,206,221
2039	89/88	72,419	17,537	89,956	97,286	97,286	-7,330	2,961	1,251,342
2040	90/89	73,990	18,305	92,295	100,222	100,222	-7,927	3,156	1,298,508
2041	91/90	75,602	18,915	94,517	103,209	103,209	-8,692	3,316	1,347,880
2042	92/91	77,256	19,512	96,768	106,269	106,269	-9,501	3,460	1,399,620
2043	93/92	78,952	20,090	99,042	109,425	109,425	-10,383	3,608	1,453,880

Bruce Larsen

For Bill and Susan, converting $250,000 of their IRA to a Roth made sense. They have an ending investments balance of $1,453,880 compared to the ending investments balance of $1,034,283 pre-conversion. The investments balance is made up of $85,644 in non-IRA savings, $198,142 in their traditional IRAs, and $1,170,094 in Roth IRAs. This is a much better composition of assets for whoever inherits their estate, which will be discussed further in a later chapter.

The total taxes they will pay over their lifetimes is $106,604 compared to $212,897 so they won on both counts. They had more in end-of-life investments and paid less taxes.

While their total taxes were $51,172 to do the conversion, they also had to cover their living expenses the year of the conversion, which resulted in their spending down all of their non-IRA savings. For most people this is an uncomfortable prerequisite. They have the option to maintain an amount in their savings and reduce the conversion amount.

The primary reason this worked out so well for Bill and Susan is the reduction in the required minimum distributions they will have to take. This is especially important when Susan is filing as a single taxpayer after Bill passes away. Of course, none of us has an expiration date, so even the best analysis isn't foolproof.

Another consideration when analyzing a Roth conversion is to look at the break-even age. Because you initially have to pay out more in taxes to get the conversion completed, your total investments balance will initially be less than had you not done a conversion. If you compare the "Total Investments" columns of the two spreadsheets, you see that the Roth conversion results in a higher total investment balance in year 2032 when Bill is 82 and Susan is 81.

Once the determination is made that a conversion can benefit you, it is then a matter of fine tuning the analysis to see if the initial projection can be improved. When we look at Bill and Susan's cash flows, we see that they won't have Social Security starting for two years so it made sense to spread the Roth conversion over two years. Thus, they don't move up so high on the tax brackets for the conversion taxes. While this makes logical sense, it actually makes very little difference to Bill and Susan due to the way their taxes are bracketed—for some people it could make a large difference.

Roth Conversion Rules

There are no income limitations to doing a Roth conversion—anyone can do one. Once money has been converted to a Roth, the principal can be drawn out anytime, but you must wait five years to draw out Roth earnings or you will be taxed on it. If you convert an IRA to a Roth prior to reaching age 59 ½, any amount withdrawn prior to age 59 ½ will be accessed a 10% early withdrawal penalty; the penalty goes away once five years have passed after the conversion.

You used to be able to re-characterize a Roth conversion back to an IRA if you feel you have made a mistake. You had until October 15 the year following the conversion prior to the 2018 tax changes. The ability to re-characterize, I believe, gave people—including investment professionals—a false sense of security. After all, if it turns out to be a mistake, analysts posit, one can always undo it. Some decisions, unfortunately, can't be undone. Let's look at a scary example.

Mary was single and is 50 years old in 2016. She is a highly paid advertising executive and makes $200,000 per year. She recently changed firms, and she has rolled her $600,000 401(k) to an IRA at a mutual fund company. She read somewhere that she might be better off if she converted the IRA to a Roth IRA. Mary has minimal non-IRA savings, concentrating instead on maximizing 401(k) contributions to reduce her current taxes.

Mary calls up her mutual fund company and asks if she can convert her IRA to a Roth. The representative she speaks to says she can, but she should consult with a tax advisor. She is told if she does it and decides later it was a bad idea, she can always convert it back to an IRA. Mary decides this is all the information she needs and requests that the representative send her the paperwork to do the conversion. The paperwork arrives, along with a lengthy explanation of the tax consequences that Mary immediately discards. She fills out the paperwork and sends it in, feeling she has made a very good decision.

Mary gets a call from her tax preparer on April 15, 2017 telling her she will owe an additional $246,976.63 in federal and state income taxes due to the Roth conversion. Mary decides she has probably made a big mistake. The first good fortune for Mary is that her tax preparer understands Roth conversion rules and files an extension for Mary, then walks her through what she must do to convert the Roth back to an IRA, which she does.

The second good fortune is she sent the 1099 from the mutual fund company to her tax preparer. I read about a case where, using the same numbers above, a woman threw away the 1099 with all the other stuff her fund company sent her. This woman missed the deadline to re-characterize, and because the only money she had was the money in the IRA, she had to withdraw it, and be taxed and penalized on it to pay the conversion taxes. She ended up paying over $366,000 in taxes, penalties, and interest. Bottom line – there is no longer a 'do-over' so make sure you know what you are doing before converting.

Conclusion

I hope I have demonstrated in this chapter that a Roth conversion is one of the most challenging transactions you can undertake in tax planning for your retirement. It doesn't help that there really aren't any good tools available for the do-it-yourself planner. Even the tools most advisory firms have at their disposal are severely lacking. The decision generally comes down to an uneducated guess.

A general rule of thumb is that if your projected IRA required minimum distributions are expected to exceed your income need, and if you have sufficient non-IRA savings to cover the taxes and your living expenses the year (or years) that you will do a Roth conversion, it generally makes sense to do so. As you have seen in this chapter, there are many variables in the analysis so this is only a very general rule.

Chapter 7 – Annuities

It seems among investors and advisors annuities are either loved or hated. The subject of this book is taxes so I don't want to get into a discussion on the merits of one investment instrument over another, other than to say if a generally available annuity has been approved for sale in every state, 50 state insurance commissions must agree that the annuity is appropriate for somebody.

I would caution investors who are advised to put all of their savings and investments into an annuity. As you have seen throughout previous chapters, our retirement cash flow needs tend to vary over time. Most annuities are designed to provide a consistent cash flow, which may or may not be appropriate for some cash flow needs. Most people will need to have more than one cash flow source in place to cover all their needs.

From a tax standpoint, there are two broad categories of annuities: qualified and non-qualified. A *qualified annuity* is an annuity held in some type of retirement plan account, either an IRA, an employer sponsored plan or a Roth IRA. A *non-qualified annuity* is an annuity that is held outside a retirement plan account; the investment in a non-qualified annuity is made with after-tax money.

Annuities can be further categorized as *immediate* (you start taking money out immediately) or *deferred* (you plan to take the money out later). The way an annuity is invested is another way to categorize it. There are *variable annuities*, which invest in subaccounts that are similar to mutual funds. *Fixed annuities* are invested at a fixed interest rate. *Fixed/indexed annuities* can be either invested in a fixed interest account or in a subaccount that provides the return of an index, such as the S & P 500® Index, subject to caps or participation rates (when the index experiences a negative return, the return of the subaccount is zero).

Annuities can also provide a wide range of enhanced income or death benefits. For instance, a variable annuity may provide an additional rider (for an additional fee) that guarantees the income base will increase at the performance of the subaccounts or 5% each year, whichever is greater. Once the investor is ready to access income, the rider would provide an income of a set percentage (typically age-based) that can be withdrawn for the rest of the investor's life (or sometimes joint life for married couples). The amount of the withdrawal is based on the income base and will last for life, even if the value of the annuity is reduced to zero.

An enhanced death benefit annuity typically will guarantee that the death benefit will increase each year in much the same way the income base increases. Enhanced death benefits usually stop increasing at a certain age, such as age 85.

An annuity contract can be annuitized for life only—meaning payments stop once the annuitant is no longer living. Many annuities also offer joint life options, which means the payments cease when the last spouse (or other joint annuitant) dies. Some (typically fixed) annuities also offer the options of the payments continuing for a certain number of years—typically 10 to 20 years —even if both annuitants pass away.

A good way to think of an annuity is the opposite of life insurance. When you purchase life insurance, you are typically insuring against dying too young. With an annuity, you are insuring against living too long. For most annuities, either the annuitized payout or the income benefit will pay out for as long as you (and optionally your spouse) live.

Both life insurance and annuities can have disadvantages. If you live a very long time, the life insurance premiums you paid were essentially wasted, unless legacy issues are factored in. If you annuitize an annuity, and pass away at a young age, the insurance company keeps the balance. Period certain annuities and joint life annuities can partially offset the risk of dying to young. Most annuities are not annuitized. Instead, most are set up to take partial withdrawals, which can preserve some of the balance of the annuity.

Non-Qualified Annuities

The tax advantage of a non-qualified annuity is that the growth in the *non-qualified deferred annuity* (NQDA) is tax deferred. You do not pay any taxes on the earnings of the annuity until the money is withdrawn. Once withdrawals start, the first tier of money to come out of the annuity is earnings. This means you pay taxes on withdrawals from the annuity until all earnings have been withdrawn before you take out the original principal. The earnings are taxed as ordinary income. If the annuity is *annuitized*, meaning a lifetime income payout is selected, part of each distribution is withdrawal as taxable earnings while part of the withdrawal is return of principal based on an IRS calculated exclusion ratio.

An NQDA can make sense for an investor who expects to have lower taxes once he or she retires. As we have seen, most people do have lower tax rates once they retire. I have heard the argument made, that does have some merit, that you are better off investing in stocks due to the lower taxation of qualified dividends and capital gains. A case can also be made for investing in tax-free municipal bonds. These arguments hold up very well for people whose income is to a level that 85% of the Social Security is taxed, but they tend to break down for lower income people.

Let's look at an example. Sam and Judy are retiring at age 70. They have IRA balances of $100,000. Sam's Social Security benefit is $1,600 per month and Judy's is $2,000. Judy also has a pension of $2,000 per month. Sam and Judy have budgeted their retirement expenses at $72,000 per year.

Judy's mother recently passed away, leaving her home to Judy. Judy sold the home for $200,000, and they are trying to decide how to invest the money to supplement their retirement. Sam and Judy have no children. While they only need about $2,000 more per year over their benefits and IRA distributions, they both agree it would be nice to have substantially more so they can travel more than their budget currently allows.

Sam and Judy make appointments with three advisors to decide how to invest the $200,000. The first advisor recommends a *single premium immediate annuity*. The annuity will pay $11,500 per year as long as either of them remains alive. The advisor explains that only $4,092.59 of the distribution will be included in their taxable income. This seems like a reasonable option to Sam and Judy, but they go ahead and keep their appointments with the other two advisors.

Their next stop is at an advisor's office who specializes in municipal bonds. This advisor looks over their annuity proposal and correctly calculates that the internal rate of return on the annuity is 3%. He tells them he can find tax exempt bonds paying the same rate of return. A combination of the $6,000 in annual interest, plus depletion of the portfolio over time, can provide them the same lifetime income with an added advantage that they are not giving up control of their investment asset—they can always change their strategy later with the remaining principal. He goes on to tell them, "This is a much more tax friendly method of investing than an annuity."

Judy asks, "What happens if we live longer than expected?"

The advisor tells them when the money is gone—it is gone.

The third advisor is a proponent of stock investing. He tells them he is fairly confident he can get them a 6% rate of return, net after fees. He tells them that about half of the return will be in the form of qualified dividends and the other half will come from long-term capital gains. He points out that this strategy will allow them to take the same distribution as the annuity while also slightly growing their principal over time. Sam and Judy ask what happens if the market goes down. At this point, the explanation gets a little murky as the advisor explains that dividend-paying stocks tend to hold up better than growth stocks during weak markets, that they are still getting the dividend during a downturn, and that during periods of good markets they will have an even higher return than projected.

Sam says, "So, can you guarantee you can get us the $11,500 every year?"

If the advisor is truthful, his answer is "no." He goes on to tell them, "Everyone knows that you pay less in taxes on qualified dividends and capital gains so you will pay less in taxes investing with me than by using an annuity."

At this point, Sam and Judy are not convinced what to do with their money. They decide that since there certainly seem to be tax consequences to their decision they should make an appointment with their tax advisor, Sally, to see if she can give them some insight.

Sally first calculates what their retirement tax picture will look like without investing the $200,000. Sam and Judy's net after tax income will be $69,107 after paying federal taxes of $1,741.07. Sally explains to them that only 24% of their Social Security benefit will be included in their taxable income. This tends to take away the tax advantages of the investing strategies they were looking at since, regardless of the investments tax characterizations, all will increase the taxation of their Social Security.

Sally prepared the following chart, showing how each strategy will affect their taxes.

			Options for Inherited Money			
Strategy	Annual Distribution	Percent Taxable	Ordinary Taxable Income	Cap Gain Qual Div Income	Factored into Soc Sec Taxation	Additional Taxes on Income
Single Premium Immediate Annuity	11,500.00	35.59%	4,092.59	-	4,092.59	1,093.72
3% Double Tax Exempt Municipal Bonds	11,500.00	0.00%	-	-	6,000.00	723.03
Stock Portfolio, 3% Yield, 3% Growth	11,500.00	104.35%	-	12,000.00	12,000.00	1,488.03

Now that Sam and Judy understand the tax ramifications of their decision, they are in a much better position to move forward. They are surprised, however, that the stock portfolio stratagem results in the least desirable tax outcome, and they wonder if the stock advisor was being dishonest with them or just didn't know how taxes work.

Once again, this is a book about taxes, not investments, so I will leave it up to the reader to decide which strategy makes the most sense for Sam and Judy. Getting on my soapbox, I would just add that a good advisor should have discussed all three approaches (or more) and given Sam and Judy several options to consider. It would most likely make sense to split the investment over more than one strategy.

One final note on non-qualified annuities. Non-qualified annuities are subject to the same early withdrawal penalties as IRAs. If you plan to take the money out before 59 ½, you should not put your money in a non-qualified annuity. The penalty evaporates if the NQDA becomes annuitized.

Qualified Annuities

The tax consequences of qualified annuities (held in retirement accounts) are plain and simple. Everything coming out of an IRA is taxable. It makes no difference how the retirement account is invested—every distribution will be taxed as ordinary income, unless it is a Roth, in which case none of the distribution is taxable provided the 5-year rule is followed.

Annuities in IRAs can be very helpful from a legacy planning standpoint. The "I" in IRA stands for individual. This can be problematic if the majority of the tax-deferred assets are held by one spouse. Many of the enhanced benefits offered by annuities apply to both spouses, regardless of who owns the annuity. For instance, several annuities with income benefits offer a long-term care rider that increases the benefit if either spouse requires skilled nursing care, regardless of whose IRA holds the annuity.

For passing on assets to children, the enhanced death benefits can also be attractive. I know of one variable annuity that will guarantee to pay to your heirs the amount in the annuity at age 70, provided you never take out more than the required minimum distribution. For example, let's look at a retiree having $500,000 in their IRA at age 70 and earning a net rate of return of 4%. Their lifetime distributions (assuming they pass away at 90) would be $540,291, and the ending value of the IRA would be $368,255.59. Having the enhanced death benefit rider would instead make the estate value of the IRA the original $500,000.

Other uses of annuities in IRAs are for income certainty. As an advisor, I often work with my clients to determine what the bare minimum cash flow needed is. If this amount is not covered by Social Security and/or pensions, it can make sense to place some of their tax-deferred investments in an annuity with a guaranteed income benefit so we know the basics are taken care of.

Conclusion

Many investors have a preconceived notion that annuities are bad. I don't believe there are any bad annuities, but I do strongly believe that many investments in annuities are inappropriate for a particular investor. As I have pointed out, there is a wide range of options in the annuity world that can add certainty, where needed, in a retirement income plan.

Annuities are simply a form of insurance. Ultimately, any type of insurance (car, home, life, etc.) is simply a way to transfer risk from yourself or your family to an insurance company. If you are concerned about running out of money in retirement, it may make sense for you to eliminate the risk by using an annuity as part of your investment portfolio.

Just because a non-qualified annuity generates ordinary income does not always mean that it will cause higher taxation than other investment devices. Like all decisions regarding taxes, you should combine the result of the annuity decision with results of the other variables in the plan in order to determine accurately what the tax consequences really are.

Chapter 8 – Life Insurance

There is an almost unlimited variety of life insurance policies available. I am going to limit my discussion primarily to the taxation of life insurance and to the uses for life insurance in retirement cash flow planning.

Purposes of Life Insurance

The most basic purpose of life insurance is to provide for your family if you die too early. I am a proponent of life insurance for young, growing families. If one of the working parents passes away at an early age, a lifetime of income is lost. Even if one of the spouses stays at home to take care of the kids and manage the household, that spouse's life should be insured as well—possibly to an even greater extent—because help would have to be hired if that parent is no longer around.

For young people *term life insurance* is usually appropriate. Term life insurance provides coverage for a specified period of time; five, ten, twenty years, etc. For young people it is fairly inexpensive, and the premium becomes more expensive as people age. Almost all life insurance premiums are also based on the health of the individual at the time the policy was placed in force. Most people can gradually reduce the policy's amount of coverage over time since as we near retirement we have less income to replace.

A secondary use of life insurance is to provide an inheritance. If a couple enters retirement with more in assets that they reasonably expect to need over their lifetimes, it often makes good tax sense to move some of their assets into life insurance policies, as will become clear once I explain how taxes work with life insurance.

In years past, another important use of life insurance was to provide liquid funds to pay inheritance taxes. Now that the estate exclusion is over $11 million dollars per person, very few people have to pay estate taxes. When I entered my financial advisor career in 1998, the exclusion was only $625,000 so a much larger number of estates were subject to estate taxes.

For those people using life insurance to provide an inheritance, permanent life insurance, often called *whole life*, is most appropriate. This type of insurance, due to the lifelong coverage, is more expensive than term life insurance.

Permanent life insurance can also provide replacement income for lost benefits if a person with large benefits predeceases a spouse. For Social Security benefits, the surviving spouse receives the higher of the two benefits, unless the survivor has a pension from non-Social Security covered earnings, e.g., some state and federal employees. If no Social Security survivor benefit is available, it may be worth exploring life insurance to replace the benefit.

Most pensions provide the option to provide a survivor benefit, usually expressed as a percentage of the pensioner's full benefit (50%, 75%, etc.). In order to provide this benefit to a spouse, the original benefit to the pensioner is reduced. If the person receiving the benefit is in good health, it may make sense to take the full benefit and purchase life insurance to replace the survivor benefit. This may be a less expensive option than taking a reduced benefit to provide for the surviving spouse.

The death benefit a beneficiary receives from a life insurance policy is excluded from income—it is totally tax free. This makes life insurance one of the most efficient ways to pass an inheritance to heirs. We will examine some other creative ways to do this later.

If you have built up cash value in a life insurance policy, you can typically access this money tax free by borrowing the money from the policy. Borrowing from life insurance cash value can be an effective retirement cash flow strategy, but it typically only works well for very high net worth people. If loans are excessive, and not repaid, it is possible for the policy to lapse, which will result in all loans exceeding premiums paid to become taxable in the year the policy lapses.

The rest of this chapter will examine several uses of life insurance for retirees.

Excess Non-Qualified Assets

Let's go back to Bill and Julie Lesley from Chapter 1. Their financial advisor, Pam, advised them to delay their Social Security until age 70, spending down some of their savings to bridge the gap between age 66 and 70. The Lesleys took Pam's recommendations. Their subsequent tax calculation is reproduced below:

Bill and Julie Taxes at Retirement (age 70)		
Bill's Social Security	33,201.90	
Julie's Social Security	33,201.90	
Total Social Security	66,403.80	
Excluded Social Security	(54,358.69)	
Taxable Social Security	12,045.12	
IRA Distributions	17,910.00	
Gross Income	29,955.12	
Standard Deduction	(15,100.00)	
Personal Exemptions	(8,100.00)	
Federal Taxable Income	6,755.12	
Federal Income Taxes	(675.51)	3.8%
Net Take-home Pay	83,638.29	

Julie calls Pam with some bad news. Her mother has just passed away. The mother had been living on Social Security and a military survivor pension from her husband, Julie's father, who had died several years ago. Julie's mom had a savings balance of $25,000 and the family home, valued at $400,000, paid for.

Pam is an only child. She will inherit all of her mother's estate.

Bill and Julie have discussed the inheritance. They are very comfortable with the income they are receiving and decide that they would like to preserve the value of the mother's estate to pass on to their children. They feel this will allow them not to worry about possibly depleting their own assets throughout

Bruce Larsen

retirement since it will leave a nice amount to go to the kids. Bill and Julie schedule a meeting with Pam to get her thoughts on what to do with the $425,000 after the house is sold.

"It's nice to see you both again. I'm sorry for your loss," Pam says as she gets them both seated in her office.

"Well, she lived a great life and I'm glad she went peacefully, not like my father who spent his last three years in the nursing home took almost all of their savings to pay for his care," Julie tells Pam.

"I'm sure your mother was pleased knowing she was able to leave something for you," says Pam.

"Yes," Julie says. "Bill and I have talked it over, and we have decided that since our retirement plan is working so well, we would like the inherited money to go to our two kids when we are gone. It doesn't look like we will need it."

Bill says, "I'm concerned, however, that this money can cause us some tax issues along the way. Can you discuss that?"

Julie pulls up her tax calculator software and enters details of their current tax projection. She explains to them that any taxable income generated by investing the money will not only be taxed, but also will cause more of the Social Security to be taxable—basically a double hit. She shows them a before-and-after view of their projected taxes investing in a 5% (ordinary income yield), shown on the next page.

Bill and Julie Taxes at Retirment (age 70)		
	Current	New
Bill's Social Security	33,202.00	33,202.00
Julie's Social Security	33,202.00	33,202.00
Total Social Security	66,404.00	66,404.00
Excluded Social Security	(54,750.00)	(36,688.00)
Taxable Social Security	11,654.00	29,716.00
Interest from Inheritance		21,250.00
IRA Distributions	17,449.00	17,449.00
Adjusted Gross Income	29,103.00	68,415.00
Standard Deduction	(26,600.00)	(26,600.00)
Personal Exemptions	-	-
Federal Taxable Income	2,503.00	41,815.00
Federal Income Taxes	(250.30)	(4,637.00)
Increased Taxes		4,386.70
Effective Rate on Inheritance Earnings		20.64%
Reinvested Amount after Taxes Paid		16,863.30
Effective After Tax Yield on Investment		3.97%
Net Take-home Pay	83,602.70	83,602.70

Bill, the bottom line guy, looks at the tax increase and says, "I thought this might be the case. Not only have we increased our taxable income, but we also have increased the amount of our taxable Social Security that is being taxed. What can we do?"

Pam outlines the first of three possibilities. The first is to invest in federally tax exempt municipal bond leveraged closed end funds. This still results in more of their Social Security being taxable, but due to the tax-free interest generated by this option, their taxes will only go up by $2,216.98 per year. This results in the net after-tax yield being 4.48%. Bill says, "That looks better—what else you got?"

Pam next explains they could put the money in a deferred variable annuity. The annuity she has in mind has a guaranteed 5% annual compounded death benefit until age 85, or the actual investment performance of the subaccounts, whichever is greater. All the earnings are tax deferred and the minimum death benefit will be $883,544 when they both turn 85. The investment will have no effect on their projected taxes unless they take the money out.

Bill says, "Now you're talking. I don't mind helping the kids, but I don't want to be clobbered with taxes to do it."

Julie says, "Okay, that sounds pretty good, but what if we need the money? I think about what long term care cost my father had—we don't have enough money if the same happens to one of us."

To this, Pam explains that they could use an annuity that grows a living benefit at the same rate as the death benefit. This option requires that they give up the guaranteed death benefit. The income benefit would be $44,177 at age 85 and would double to $88,354 if either of them were ever confined to a nursing home. Because of the large health care deduction they would receive, very little taxes would be due on the distributions.

Julie says, "Guess we can't have our cake and eat it too. If we need it, the kids won't get it. Of course, they will get our house, so I guess that would have to be enough. You mentioned three options, what is next?"

Pam tells them that since they are both in good health, they should consider a life insurance policy. The life insurance policy should reach about the same value as the annuity and, best of all, when the Lesleys pass, the entire proceeds would go to their children tax free. All the gain in the annuity would be taxable to the kids as they take distributions.

Another advantage of the life policy is that it has an accelerated death benefit rider. This means if either Bill or Julie need long-term care, they can take out the death benefit to pay for it. One final advantage of the life policy is that they could borrow out some of the cash value if they needed it, provided the policy is set up properly. Bill wants more explanation.

Pam tells him that if the policy is overfunded, to make it more like an investment than a life insurance policy, it is no longer technically a life policy, but it is considered by the IRS to be a *modified endowment contract*. If this happens, it is taxed the same as an annuity if Bill or Julie accesses funds. If inherited by their children, it can be tax free.

Bill says, "Okay, my brain is overloading. What should we do?"

Pam tells them that she has been speaking in generalizations about the various options. She tells them that she needs to do some work to put them in the best position possible. She restates their goals, which are:

- Preserve and grow the funds to leave to the kids
- Don't screw up the Lesley's current tax projection
- Provide liquidity, if needed, to cover long term care if either needs to go into a nursing home

When they meet the following week, it is most likely that a life insurance policy will meet their needs.

Excess Qualified Funds

While most people will need to squeeze everything they can out of their IRAs and other retirement assets, I do occasionally encounter people who have too much money in their IRAs, and a Roth conversion wouldn't make sense. These are typically frugal people, who have large pensions along with high Social Security benefits. Once they get to retirement age, the RMDs they have to take aren't needed, and yet the RMDs burden them with additional taxes.

An example always works best. Ted and Mary Sampson are both turning 70 ½ this year. Mary was a school teacher, and she now receives a taxable pension of $70,000 per year. Her earnings were not subject to Social Security, so she gets no Social Security, nor will she receive a survivor benefit from Ted's Social Security due to the *government pension offset*. The government pension offset reduces a spousal Social Security benefit by two thirds of the pension benefit, so in Mary's case, a Social Security survivor benefit would be reduced by $46,666.66.

Ted put in twenty years in the Air Force, retiring as a Major, and is receiving a pension of $40,000. Members of the armed forces fully participate in the Social Security system. Ted spent the last twenty-five years of his career working for a government contractor. He has Social Security benefits of $32,400. Ted also has an IRA balance of $600,000. The IRA is invested very conservatively, earning about 4% per year. Our financial advisor, Pam, also works with the Sampsons. They schedule a meeting to find out how their tax projection is going to change once the RMDs start.

Pam starts the meeting by showing the Sampsons what changes occur in their tax projection, shown on the next page. She also shows them how life insurance can maintain, and possibly enhance, the value of their estate.

Ted and Mary, before and after RMD's		
	Current	New
Ted's Social Security	32,400.00	32,400.00
Ted's Military Pension	40,000.00	40,000.00
Mary's Pension	70,000.00	70,000.00
Total Social Security	102,400.00	102,400.00
Excluded Social Security	4,860.00	4,860.00
Taxable Social Security	27,540.00	29,715.68
IRA Distributions	-	21,818.18
Adjusted Gross Income	137,540.00	139,715.68
Standard Deduction	(26,600.00)	(26,600.00)
Personal Exemptions	-	-
Federal Taxable Income	110,940.00	113,115.68
Federal Income Taxes	(16,286.00)	(24,055.00)
Increased Taxes		7,769.00
Net Take-home Pay	86,114.00	100,163.18

Ted says, "Well, I guess it is nice to have some more income, even though we will be paying more in taxes. We really don't need the money—I was hoping our daughter could inherit my IRA—she isn't a very good saver, so it would really help her out when she retires."

Pam says, "Sure, nothing wrong with more money. The problem is, the taxes you pay will increase each year as the amount you need to take out increases. And, if you both live a good long life, there is going to be very little left in the IRA to bequeath to your daughter, Jill."

Mary says, "Since we don't need the money, couldn't we invest the excess into something we could leave for Jill? We really want to take care of her."

Pam tells them she understands but points out they will have to pay taxes on the earnings of the new investment strategy.

Ted, a very direct person due to his military background, says, "Okay, let's cover the main points we are dealing with. As you know, I like as much certainty as I can get in a plan. We don't need this money, and we want to provide as much as possible to Jill. Is there anything we can do today to provide a smooth tax ride while using this IRA to help Jill as much as possible?"

Pam tells them she understands where they are coming from and schedules a meeting for the following Monday to review what they can do after she has had a chance to run some numbers.

Monday rolls around and the Sampsons are back at Pam's office. Pam tells them she thinks she has a solution. After some small talk, Pam gets to the point: "Okay, bear with me. I'm going to propose that we take <u>more</u> out of the IRA than the required minimum distribution. The nice thing about the distribution is that it will not change over your lifetimes, so this fits Ted's desire to provide certainty in the plan. We will pay the taxes on the distributions—can't avoid that—but the remaining amount will be used to purchase a joint second to die life insurance policy. This policy, assuming no detrimental health issues are discovered during the underwriting, will provide Jill at tax-free death benefit of $1,015,000—that is over $400,000 more than is currently in your IRA."

Ted says, "Show me how this works." Pam shows them the diagram below.

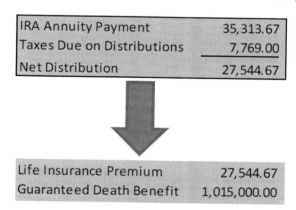

IRA Annuity Payment	35,313.67
Taxes Due on Distributions	7,769.00
Net Distribution	27,544.67

| Life Insurance Premium | 27,544.67 |
| Guaranteed Death Benefit | 1,015,000.00 |

Pam explains that the entire balance of the IRA is invested in a single premium immediate annuity. The payments are guaranteed for the duration of both Ted and Mary's lives. While their taxes will go up, the taxes will be paid on the distribution before the life insurance premium is paid, neutralizing the Sampson's current tax obligation.

Ted says, "So effectively, our own after tax-income doesn't change, but instead of Jill getting what is left of my $600,000 IRA, she gets over $1 million in life insurance." Pam assents and points out that if Jill were to inherit the IRA, she would have to pay taxes on the IRA distributions, where contrariwise the amount coming out of the insurance policy is tax free.

Mary is concerned that Jill might just blow the money so Pam suggests that they meet with an estate attorney to develop a plan to protect Jill from her herself. We will discuss this in more detail later.

Using Cash Value Policies to Fund Retirement

There are many books on the subject of a "tax-free retirement." While it is possible to get there, as I'll demonstrate in one of the last chapters of this book, there isn't any free lunch. As touched on briefly at the beginning of this chapter, the strategy using life insurance starts by funding a cash value (whole life) insurance policy during your working years. Once you retire, you can then theoretically take tax-free loans out of the policy for the rest of your life. Once you pass away, your heirs get whatever is left in the policy tax free.

As with all strategies, you have what I term the "The Good, The Bad, and The Ugly." "The Bad" is that contributions to a life insurance policy aren't tax deductible. Typically, this means that the strategy only works well for people who have maximized their contributions to deductible retirement savings plans and earn too much money to qualify for Roth IRA contributions.

"The Good" of this strategy is that you absolutely can take cash-free loans out of the policy for the rest of your life, assuming that the return earned by the cash value was sufficient to increase the amount of the value to provide for the loans.

"The Ugly" part of this strategy is that your returns may be lower than expected. If this happens, there may not be enough cash value to support any loans. In severe cases, the return may be so low that not only can't you take out loans, but you must begin paying premiums again to keep it from lapsing.

I want to stress that I am not against this strategy, but you need to go into a cash value plan with your eyes wide open. Some questions I as a client would ask are:

- What is the rate of return we need to get to make this work?
- What happens if the return is less?
- What have been the ranges of returns in this policy on rolling 10-year periods?
- What happens, assuming worse case returns, to the policy?
- Are you, my advisor, going to be around to guide me through it in 20 years when I'm ready to get money out of this thing?

The last question is the big one. Life insurance policies carry some of the highest commissions out there so there can be incentive for agents to oversell them. Most plans involve paying premiums over a set period of time, typically seven years. Then the policy is left alone for anywhere from five to ten years before policy loans begin. The agent who sold you the policy may not be around to guide you through the distribution phase.

As with most strategies, I strongly encourage you not to put all of your money in one instrument. I also encourage you to run all of your strategies through one point of contact—one financial advisor who can watch all the moving parts of your retirement plan.

Conclusion

As I hope I have pointed out, there can be some very good uses of life insurance in a well-constructed retirement plan. Life insurance is a very long-term investment, and you need to consider carefully all the good and bad points before entering into a contract.

Chapter 9 – Smart Use of Leverage in Retirement

People generally have a goal to enter retirement debt free. While I see nothing wrong with having this as a goal, I don't think you should let the IRS hit you over the head to get there.

As long as your debt is at a reasonable interest rate, it can prove to be advantageous. Contrariwise, it can often be very detrimental to pay off a large balance just so you won't have a monthly payment in retirement. Recall, there are no absolutes. Freedom from debt at retirement is certainly not a boon universally. It can make very good sense to pay off debt going into retirement, but not absolutely.

Also, keep in mind that fixed-rate debt, such as most mortgages, have constant payments. As your Social Security and required minimum distributions increase, the fixed payment amount makes up a smaller percentage of your cash flow over time.

Pay Off Mortgage

Let's look at a real-world scenario. Jake and Cathy Jones were well on their way to getting their mortgage paid off prior to retiring at age 70. Unfortunately, their daughter, Sue, didn't get the scholarship they had hoped for to get her through the private college she had her heart set on. Jake and Cathy had struggled to pay off their student loans and didn't want Sue to have the same burden. They decided to refinance their house to cover her loans for her. Now, their first year in retirement, they decide to take money out of Cathy's 401(k) to pay off the loan.

A little background on the Jones's circumstances:
- Each has Social Security Benefits of $24,000 annually

- Cathy's IRA balance is $475,000
- Once the mortgage is paid off, they can live comfortably on $55,000 after tax annually
- They have no liquid saving—the IRA is all there is

Their current loan amortization schedule is shown below.

Year	Interest Rate	4.00%		
	Loan Balance	Annual Payment	Interest	Principle
2018	107,000	9,600	4,280	5,320
2019	101,680	9,600	4,067	5,533
2020	96,147	9,600	3,846	5,754
2021	90,393	9,600	3,616	5,984
2022	84,409	9,600	3,376	6,224
2023	78,185	9,600	3,127	6,473
2024	71,713	9,600	2,869	6,731
2025	64,981	9,600	2,599	7,001
2026	57,980	9,600	2,319	7,281
2027	50,700	9,600	2,028	7,572
2028	43,128	9,600	1,725	7,875
2029	35,253	9,600	1,410	8,190
2030	27,063	9,600	1,083	8,517
2031	18,545	9,600	742	8,858
2032	9,687	9,600	387	9,213

They tell Howard, their tax advisor, they are thinking of taking money out of Cathy's IRA to pay off the $107,000 balance. They reason that since they aren't able to utilize the relatively small interest deduction (They file using the standard deduction.), they might as well get rid of the mortgage and reduce their yearly expenses by $9,600 per year.

Howard explains to them that they will owe a huge tax bill if they do this, and that they would then lose the income that the $107,000 could provide for them. They feel they can expect about a 7% return so they are giving up less than their payment—$7,490 earnings compared to the $9,600 payment.

Howard tells them they really need to know the ramifications of this decision before they make it. He invites them into his office to go over the ramifications of their plan.

When they arrive at Howard's office, he starts by eating a little crow. He says, "Taking that large distribution from your IRA will cause 85 percent of your Social Security to be taxed in the year you take it. Currently, only 11 percent of it is taxed. Also, your Medicare premiums will go up due to the high income for the year. That being said, when I run the numbers, you are absolutely correct that it makes sense to pay off the mortgage despite my initial reservations." He shows them his comparison chart below.

Jake and Cathy - Pay off Analysis			
	Current	Payoff Year	New
Jake's Social Security	24,000.00	24,000.00	24,000.00
Cathy's Social Security	24,000.00	24,000.00	24,000.00
Total Social Security	48,000.00	48,000.00	48,000.00
Excluded Social Security	42,500.00	7,200.00	45,023.00
Taxable Social Security	5,500.00	40,800.00	2,470.00
IRA Distributions (4%)	19,000.00	149,000.00	13,953.00
Adjusted Gross Income	24,500.00	189,800.00	16,423.00
Standard Deduction	(26,600.00)	(26,600.00)	(26,600.00)
Personal Exemptions	-	-	-
Federal Taxable Income	-	163,200.00	-
Federal Income Taxes	-	(32,307.00)	-
Mortgage Payment	9,600.00	107,000.00	-
Net Take-home Pay	57,400.00	57,693.00	61,953.00

Howard goes on to explain that the reason this works for them is that, after the payoff, only a very small portion of their Social Security will be taxable so they will owe no federal taxes. Howard goes on to say that a payoff from IRA funds typically doesn't work out this way, but he is glad that it does for them. He prints the copy of his analysis for them to take to their financial advisor who predictably won't be happy to see them liquidate $149,000 of their IRA balance.

I have a confession to make. When I started to work out the Jake and Kathy illustration, I had the same preconceived opinion as Howard that it would make more sense not to pay the mortgage off. Let's look at another example to see how it works out.

Car Purchase

Millie Conner is 72 and needs a new car. She thought the car she went into retirement with at age 65 would get her all the way through retirement. Now that she is retired, she has become the unofficial taxi driver for her four grandchildren. She also has been doing more travel than expected out of state. Millie's car is putting on a lot of miles.

Millie has found the car she likes. With the trade-in value of her old car, she needs $30,000.00 for the purchase. The dealership is offering her 2.90% financing for five years. She realizes this is a great deal, but she has gotten used to not having a car payment and would prefer to pay cash.

Millie has an IRA valued at $625,000. She is taking 4% distributions from the IRA ($25,000 annually). Millie also has annual Social Security of $26,000. Millie needs about $41,000 annually to cover all of her expenses. Her current tax calculation is shown on the following table (Fortunately, her children pay for her gas when she is driving kids to soccer practice, etc.).

Millie - Car Purchase		
	Current	
Cathy's Social Security	26,000.00	
Excluded Social Security	18,100.00	
Taxable Social Security	7,900.00	30%
IRA Distributions (4%)	25,000.00	
Adjusted Gross Income	32,900.00	
Standard Deduction	(13,600.00)	
Personal Exemptions	--	
Federal Taxable Income	19,300.00	
Federal Income Taxes	(2,126.00)	
Net Take-home Pay	48,874.00	

Notice that only 30% of Millie's Social Security it being taxed. For most of her income, she is in the 10% bracket, slightly crossing over into the 15%

bracket. In order to pay $30,000 for the car, she assumes she needs to take $30,000 extra out of her IRA; and, because she is getting more than she needs now, she can use the $7,000 extra to pay the taxes. What actually needs to happen for Millie to net her $41,000 per year is shown on the table below.

Millie - Car Purchase - No Financing		
	Current	Next Year
Social Security	26,000.00	26,000.00
Excluded Social Security	3,900.00	18,807.00
Taxable Social Security	22,100.00	7,193.00
IRA Distributions (4%)	55,000.00	24,168.00
Adjusted Gross Income	77,100.00	31,361.00
Standard Deduction	(13,600.00)	(13,600.00)
Personal Exemptions	-	-
Federal Taxable Income	63,500.00	17,761.00
Federal Income Taxes	(9,910.00)	(1,941.00)
Car Purchase	(30,000.00)	-
Net Take-home Pay	41,090.00	48,227.00

Because 85% of Millie's Social Security is now taxable, she has a much larger tax bill than she expected. She has to distribute $55,000 from her IRA to have the same net take-home pay she had before.

If she finances the car at 2.9% over five years, her annual payments will be $6,531.95. Over five years, that totals $32,659.75, so she is only paying $2,659.75 in interest. This is much better than paying additional taxes of $7,784 the year she pays cash for the car. Taking the big distribution from her IRA will also result in slightly lower lifetime payments.

Because Millie has determined she can live on $41,000 net per year, she doesn't have to take additional distributions from her IRA and, once the car is paid off, she goes back to the same tax status she was in before. Her projection with financing is shown on the next page.

Millie - Car Purchase - 2.9% Financing		
	Years 1-5	Paid off
Social Security	26,000.00	26,000.00
Excluded Social Security	18,100.00	18,100.00
Taxable Social Security	7,900.00	7,900.00
IRA Distributions (4%)	25,000.00	25,000.00
Adjusted Gross Income	32,900.00	32,900.00
Standard Deduction	(13,600.00)	(13,600.00)
Personal Exemptions	-	-
Federal Taxable Income	19,300.00	19,300.00
Federal Income Taxes	(2,126.00)	(2,126.00)
Car Payments	(6,531.95)	-
Net Take-home Pay	42,342.05	48,874.00

Currently, we are in a very low interest rate environment, so it makes financing most large purchases an even better option than if rates were normal—whatever normal is. While the difference in net take home pay is small, I would still recommend financing because Millie would be preserving more of her principle.

Most of my clients have the majority of their savings in traditional (before tax) 401(k)s and IRAs. Having tax diversification—meaning that you have a mix of traditional IRAs, non-tax-deferred savings and investments, and Roth accounts—gives people more options. If Millie, in the example above, had had the $30,000 cost of the car in a savings account or a Roth, and had she paid cash for the car, she could have averted such an ugly tax result.

If there were no tax consequences to paying cash, the decision then becomes based purely on interest rates. If you are earning more money in your savings or the Roth account, it would make sense to finance. Other factors that can influence the optimal decision for you are the amount of liquidity you have and what liquidity you want to give up on a large purchase.

Conclusion

As with many decisions involving retirement cash flow decisions, deciding to pay cash or finance a large purchase takes careful analysis. For people who have not reached the point that 85% of their Social Security is taxable, taking large distributions from an IRA can result in double taxations. Not only are you taxed more because of a larger distribution, but you also have to pay more taxes on your Social Security benefits.

Chapter 10 – Legacy Planning

This chapter will discuss the income tax issues involved in passing an estate to heirs. Most of us no longer have to be concerned about estate taxes because each individual can now exclude over $11 million from their taxable estate.

Legacy planning is an uncomfortable area of planning for most people. None of us wants to face the fact that we won't be around forever. I strongly encourage you to do the planning necessary, despite the discomfort, in order to ensure a smooth estate distribution. I have seen many families torn apart because of the lack of a coherent, articulated estate strategy. Again, I'm here to talk about income taxes, but I would I would like to give you my main reason for developing an estate plan.

The primary goal of estate planning is to avert a financial quagmire for your kids or grandkids to sort out.

Okay, now that I have that off my chest, let's dive into my favorite subject—taxes!

Death of a Spouse

Losing a spouse is obviously a very traumatic experience. To add insult to injury, the surviving spouse will most likely end up in a worse tax situation than he or she was in prior to losing the spouse. Several undesirable tax implications happen to survivors the year following the death of a spouse.

First, your standard deduction is cut in half. In 2018, married filing jointly couples 65 and older have a standard deduction of $26,600. Once one spouse passes, the standard deduction in the year after death is reduced to $13,600.

The next thing pushing a less desirable tax outcome is that the calculation of the extent of Social Security that will be taxed moves to a single filer table, rather than joint. We aren't done yet. The final blow is that your taxes are now taxed at single tax brackets rather than joint, which produce roughly one half the tax relief of joint brackets.

At first, this may not seem to matter too much. After all, the smaller of the two Social Security benefits stops so income should be lower. This would be fine if all you were receiving is Social Security, but most retirees are also taking distributions from multiple tax-deferred accounts. Assuming two spouses are the same age when one passes, the survivor must take the same amount out in required minimum distributions as the joint couple were distributing.

Let's look at an example. Cliff and Suzy Carter are both 74 years old. They have a comfortable retirement with net disposable income of $96,608. Their tax calculation is shown below.

Cliff and Suzy Carter		
	Current	
John's Social Security	31,285.00	
Mary's Social Security	20,149.00	
Total Social Security	51,434.00	
Excluded Social Security	16,774.00	
Taxable Social Security	34,660.00	67.4%
IRA Distributions RMD's	52,000.00	
Adjusted Gross Income	86,660.00	
Standard Deduction	(26,600.00)	
Personal Exemptions	-	
Federal Taxable Income	60,060.00	
Federal Income Taxes	(6,826.00)	11.4%
Net Take-home Pay	96,608.00	

They have a federal tax liability of $6,826, which represents 11.4% of their taxable income. When the taxes are calculated on their total cash flow of $103,434 (total Social Security plus IRA RMDs), the percentage on cash flow is only 6.6%. Now let's look at what happens to Suzy's taxes the year after Cliff passes away.

(I will be killing off the husband first in all examples in this chapter—statistically, that is how it generally works out. Hope the guys out there are fine with this.)

Suzy Carter		
	Current	
John's Social Security	31,285.00	
Mary's Social Security	-	
Total Social Security	31,285.00	
Excluded Social Security	4,693.00	
Taxable Social Security	26,592.25	85.0%
IRA Distributions RMD's	52,000.00	
Adjusted Gross Income	78,592.25	
Standard Deduction	(13,600.00)	
Personal Exemptions	-	
Federal Taxable Income	64,992.25	
Federal Income Taxes	(10,238.00)	15.8%
Net Take-home Pay	73,047.00	

This is a somewhat ugly position to be in. Even though Suzy has lost one Social Security benefit (the surviving spouse generally gets the higher of the two benefits) and has less money coming in, she will have to pay about $3,400 more in federal taxes. Suzy ends up with about 76% of the disposable income—even though she is paying more taxes.

Is there anything that Suzy can do? At this point, not much. You may remember from Chapter 5, Roth Conversions, one of the reasons to consider converting is so the surviving spouse will have some tax free-income. The Carters, unfortunately, didn't do any Roth conversions and now that Suzy is in the single tax brackets it probably wouldn't make sense to do a conversion. I hope Suzy can live on 76% of Cliff's and her prior income.

Beneficiary Designations

Let's take this example a little further. Assuming the entire IRA was Cliff's, Suzy will be in good shape if Cliff designated her the primary beneficiary of the IRA. If Cliff didn't name her and instead entered "My Spouse" on the beneficiary form for his IRA, Suzy could only spread the IRA distributions over five years.

If the $52,000 distribution is just the RMD, the balance of the IRA would be $1,283,950. If the beneficiary designation had said "My Spouse," Suzy could spread the distributions out over the next five years, or $256,790 annually. She could take it all out at once, which would make things worse—her best option is to spread it out as much as she can. This scenario gets really ugly. She has a tax bill of over $70,000 annually for the next five years!

If you haven't had this explained to you, or if you haven't found it out with your own research, you are probably asking yourself what is the difference between Cliff's naming "My Spouse" instead of "Suzy Carter"—aren't both referring to the same person? The IRS has taken the position that only a *named beneficiary* has the option of lifetime distributions when inheriting an IRA. If a beneficiary is not named, the IRA must be distributed over a period of not more than five years. I don't make the rules; I'm just trying to help you navigate them.

Let's move on to taxes on other, non-IRA inherited assets.

Receiving a 'Gift' or an 'Inheritance'

You are generally in a better tax scenario if you inherit an asset than if you receive an asset as a gift. The difference lies in how cost basis is determined. If you receive an asset as a gift, your cost basis is the *fair market value* (FMV) of the asset on the date of the gift or the donor's cost basis, whichever is less. Once the asset is sold, you pay capital gains on the difference between the sale proceeds and cost basis.

If you inherit an asset, your cost basis is the value on the date of death (or six months after in special circumstances). Let's look at a couple of examples to make sure this concept is clear.

In the first example, your father purchased 500 shares of a stock at $10 per share. The stock is now worth $30 dollars per share. The unrealized gain is

$10,000 ($30 less $10 times 500 shares). If your father gives you the shares, your cost basis would be his cost basis because the cost basis of a gift is the FMV or the donor's basis, whichever is less. If you sell the stock, you will owe taxes on $10,000 gain.

If your father passes away and you inherit the stock, you are allowed to step-up the cost basis to the value on date of death. With the step-up in basis of $30 per share, you could sell the stock and have no taxable gain.

Now let's turn the situation around. Let's hypothesize your father bought the 500 shares for $30, and it is now worth $10. If he gives you the stock, your basis is again FMV or your father's cost basis, whichever is less, so your basis is $10.00. Your basis would be the same if you inherited the stock—FMV on date of death.

You may now assume that it doesn't matter how an asset with a loss is transferred—you end up with the same cost basis, right? That is correct, but think back to your father—by transferring an asset with an unrealized loss he was never able to realize the loss, nor were you. Assets with unrealized losses should be sold by the owner, if possible.

I have helped several clients settle estates of their parents. It always surprises me to see unrealized losses on their brokerage statements—losses they could have realized while alive and used to offset other taxable gains or up to $3,000 of ordinary income.

Okay, now that we have a general understanding of cost basis, let's move on to the titling of assets.

Titling of Assets

I'm going to address several mistakes that I have seen people make when organizing their estates. Most of these mistakes are a direct result of do-it-yourself estate planning. It should come as no surprise that I strongly encourage everyone, even those with modest estates, to consult with an estate attorney rather than taking short cuts.

Over Use of Joint Tenancy

Two or more people can own a property either as joint tenants or as tenants in common. There are important differences between these two ownership types with respect to what happens when a co-owner dies.

Tenants in common may have different ownership interests. For instance, tenant 1 may own 25% of a property with tenant 2 owning 75%. Joint tenants, on the other hand, hold equal shares of the property. The default ownership characterization for married couples is joint tenancy in some states, and tenancy in common in others.

There are several reasons for married couples to own property as joint tenants rather than as tenants in common. The best reason to own property in joint tenancy is that it avoids probate. At the death of one spouse the remaining spouse becomes the sole owner. If the property had been owned as tenants in common, the share owned by the deceased spouse is included in the deceased spouse's estate and would most likely have to go through probate.

Joint tenancy is a familiar term for most people. Most couples have some, if not all, of their assets (other than qualified accounts) in joint tenancy. This works very well, most of the time, because an unlimited amount of assets can be gifted or bequeathed to a spouse with no estate tax consequences. Passing assets to someone through joint tenancy, as mentioned above, also keeps the asset out of probate.

From a tax perspective, any assets held in joint tenancy by a couple only receive one half step-up in cost basis when one spouse passes away. For instance, consider a husband and wife who owned a stock worth $100,000 that they paid $50,000 for. Their cost basis is $50,000. If one spouse were to pass away, only one half of the cost basis would step up so the surviving spouse would have a new cost basis of $75,000. If the stock were sold, the taxable gain would be $25,000.

Can this predicament be avoided? Possibly. Let's assume the husband is in poor health. It would be to the wife's advantage to transfer the asset to sole ownership of her husband. Once he passes, her cost basis would step up to the full value of $100,000 so there would be no taxable gain if the stock were sold immediately. This asset would be included in the husband's probate estate unless he put a *transfer on death* (TOD) designation on the account, which would cause the asset to pass by contract/agreement rather than through probate and still get the step up in cost basis.

You should keep in mind that there is a one-year look-back on gifted assets; a year would have to pass for this to be considered a completed gift/transfer between the spouses for the survivor to get the full cost basis step-up.

I know it sounds somewhat cold to discuss these matters. After all, in the example above, the last thing a wife with an unwell husband wants to do is jump through hoops to save a few dollars on taxes. She probably has too much on her mind to worry about tax minimization. This is where a family member or a financial or tax advisor can possibly help.

Non-Spouse Joint Tenancy

Thorny tax issues really evolve when people pass assets to non-spouses using joint tenancy. While I don't want to get too far in the weeds on legal issues, you need to understand that joint tenancy also means joint liability. If you put a favorite grandchild on your house as a joint tenant to avoid probate, and the kid is sued, you could be forced to either sell your house or borrow against it to cover a judgement against the grandchild. If that doesn't scare you enough, let's talk about the tax issues.

Assuming the grandchild didn't have any issues putting the house in jeopardy, what does the grandchild's tax status look like when she inherits the house? Again, adding joint tenancy onto an asset is similar to gifting. The grandchild inherits your cost basis along with the house. Assuming the grandchild doesn't occupy the house, she would have a taxable gain on the sale of the home equal to the difference between the selling price and what you paid for it, plus capital improvements if records were kept.

What is a better way? Again, a TOD designation can be put on the deed in most states. This not only keeps the house out of probate, but it also allows the grandchild to step-up the cost basis. As an added bonus, none of the grandchild's liabilities can be attached to the house.

Leaving a house to a child or grandchild through joint tenancy is one of those areas that can cause hard feelings and a lot of miscommunication when it is time to settle an estate. Let's look at a really hairy scenario.

Mavis Sims is a widow with three children. She is living in an $800,000 FMV home with an adjusted basis of $250,000 (what Mavis and her husband paid for it plus documented capital improvements). Mavis lives in New Jersey. Mavis's most successful daughter, Judy, also lives in New Jersey. Her other two children, Jim and Sally, are middle-income earners living in Florida.

Mavis's only other assets, other than personal assets, are her tax-deferred accounts. She has all three children listed individually as one third beneficiaries of all her tax-deferred accounts. Mavis also has a will saying that each child gets one third of her assets, including the home.

Judy, the daughter in New Jersey, knows just enough about estate planning to be dangerous. She knows that in New Jersey an estate tax return will have to be filed if the estate is valued at over $675,000. She also realizes if the home passes through joint tenancy it would be not be included in the estate value.

Judy discusses this with her mother who decides it makes sense to put the kids on the deed as joint tenants. She calls her brother and sister in Florida who also agree it is a good idea, but they say it would be easier just to have Judy as the joint tenant so they won't have to do a "bunch of paperwork." After the mother's death, Judy will sell the house, split the money and distribute a third to each of the siblings. You know already this is a bad idea, but you might not know how bad it really is. The chart on the following page shows how Judy's taxes are effected by poor, do-it-yourself estate planning.

Mavis Sims House Sale to Settle Estate		
Judy's Gross New Jersey Earnings before Sale		250,000
Judy's Federal Taxes		58,990
Judy's New Jersey Taxes		13,736
Judy's Gross New Jersey Earnings before Sale		250,000
Judy's Capital Gain on Sale		550,000
Judy's Adjusted Gross Income		800,000
Judy's Federal Taxes		188,290
Judy's New Jersey Taxes		56,545
Additional Taxes Due Caused by Sale of House	Federal	129,300
	State	42,809
	Total	172,109
Sale Proceeds Net of Taxes Paid		627,891
Loss in Value Due to Poor Planning		172,109

The taxes Judy will have to pay on the sale would easily have covered costs for an estate attorney. After Judy meets with her tax preparer and finds out how much taxes will be paid on the sale, she calls her brother and sister. Judy lets them know that instead of getting $266,666, a third of $800,000—they will instead get $209,297 because of all the taxes she had to pay on the sale.

Judy's brother, Jim, seems to remember hearing something about getting a step-up in basis when assets are inherited so he gives an estate attorney a call. After explaining the situation, the attorney informs Jim that had they let the house pass through a living trust, or put a TOD on the deed, no taxes would have been due. Using joint tenancy did not allow for step-up in basis. The estate attorney points out the best thing they could have done was create a living trust for Mavis and titled the house to the living trust. The trust, at death, could have sold the home with no capital gains taxes due.

Jim, not at all happy, gives Judy a call. He says, "That was a great job you did on Mom's estate planning. Your great idea to be joint tenant on the house cost us each $57,369. It was your idea, so I think you should pay the taxes since my attorney says we wouldn't have had to pay them if you had done things right."

Judy, who feels terrible about how things worked out, says, "I discussed it with both of you, and you both agreed with the strategy."

Jim answers, "Yeah, but you didn't tell me how much taxes would have to be paid."

Judy says, "I didn't know how much in taxes would be due until we sold the place."

Jim replies, "Well, it was your idea; we shouldn't have to pay for something that we wouldn't have done if you hadn't told us it was a good idea." This conversation goes on and on, probably for the rest of their lives. Even the best of siblings wouldn't be happy about being clipped for $57,369 in unnecessary taxes.

Judy also has the option, if she gets tired of listening to Jim complain, to keep the entire proceeds of the sale—she was the only joint tenant, so she has no legal obligation to give her siblings any of the proceeds. The word "give" is important in the last sentence. When Judy does transfer the net proceeds to Jim and Sally she is required to file a gift tax return. The amount of the "gifts" to Jim and Sally will reduce Judy's estate exclusion when she passes away.

Most attorneys can put a very good, tax-savvy estate plan together for no more than about $5,000. When you consider the value of most estates that include a paid-for home with low basis, I think it is money well spent if for no other reason than to keep your kids talking to each other on good terms after you are gone.

Living (Revocable) Trusts

Many estate attorneys recommend creating a *living trust* and placing any assets subject to probate into the trust. You put assets into the trust simply by retitling the asset to the trust. The advantage of a living trust, if properly constructed and funded, is that probate is avoided, which generally means the estate can be settled faster and with less legal expense. I'm not going to go any further with this description but be aware that creating a living trust does nothing to alter your income taxes due.

A living trust, even if it is a *joint living trust* (between spouses) uses the Social

Security number of one of the trustees. If one spouse passes away, the trust is no longer a joint trust so, if the trust is under the Social Security number of the spouse that passes, the accounts held by the trust will have to be changed to be reported under the new trustee's Social Security number.

Almost every living trust I work with is under the husband's Social Security number. Because husbands are statistically expected to pass before their wives, I'm not sure why this is—just convention I guess. If you are working with an attorney, I would suggest you use the Social Security number of the spouse expected to live the longest—this will save administrative paperwork later.

It has been my experience that settling an estate structured as a living trust is much easier than settling an estate through a will. The only time I have seen things get difficult is when the parents name more than one successor trustee to settle the trust, such as all four kids rather than just one. Doing this causes all four kids have to agree and sign off on everything being done.

There are two other purposes of a living trust. Rather than simply distributing all of the trust assets directly to the beneficiaries (the kids) the living trust could create separate share trusts for each child. The separate trusts are creditor protected; a nice benefit lost if the proceeds are directly distributed.

A trust can also specify how distributions are made. This can help protect beneficiaries from themselves. If you have a child that you know will take his inheritance and spend it all immediately, you can have the trust specify that only a small amount is distributed on a yearly basis.

Irrevocable Trusts

An *irrevocable trust* is a "permanent" trust. It can be thought of as an irrevocable gift made by the grantor (creator) of a trust to the beneficiaries of the trust. If structured properly, the beneficiaries can receive a step-up in basis when the grantor passes away. The main use of an irrevocable trust is to pass control of assets to someone other than the grantor if the grantor is unable to manage their affairs, typically due to advanced age or disability. Typically, the grantor continues to receive trust income and have the use of trust assets, such as a home, while alive. The trust then is distributed to the beneficiaries once the grantor passes away.

An irrevocable trust can be structured so that the tax liability of any income earned by trust assets can be taxed on the grantor's tax return. This is the preferred method because you hit the top federal tax bracket for trust income at a little over $12,000 in income. An irrevocable trust, like a living trust, avoids probate.

Consolidation and Communication

This section has absolutely nothing to do with taxes, but I couldn't leave this chapter without a little common-sense advice on making estate settlement easier. If at all possible, especially later in life, you should consolidate as much of your investment assets as possible with one competent advisor.

I recently helped a client and his four siblings settle an estate of their mother. She had investments with 37 separate firms. Apparently, she had followed the adage: "don't put all your eggs in one basket." Unfortunately, none of her children had more than a vague idea where these accounts were. We basically had to leave the estate open for a year (some firms only provide yearly statements) so we could make sure we had everything accounted for. This portfolio was a nightmare to sort out.

In today's online world, many people do not receive paper statements, opting instead to receive statements via email or online access. Give some thought to how your kids would find all your stuff if both you and your wife pass away. Do they know the password to get into your email? Have you given one of your children a listing of your online accounts?

Having a trusted financial advisor, and telling your kids who he or she is, can go a long way to sorting out an estate. Most financial advisors would be happy to keep copies of your estate planning documents, and any other documents, for you so they can be released to either your successor trustee or the executor of your estate. I tell my clients to instruct heirs to contact me once they (the clients) die.

I have two bad examples of how lack of communication can cause unintended expenses. I refer to two instances (fortunately not my clients) of people who passed away with prepaid funeral plans. Neither decedent wanted his kids to have to pay for his funeral. What did both do with the paperwork on their funeral plans? They both put them in their safety deposit boxes and didn't tell anyone about them. Once they passed, their kids got together and paid for a funeral. Then, as is typical, a few days later, the executor opened the safety deposit boxes and found the unused plans—they aren't refundable.

Conclusion

Congratulations on finishing this chapter. I know this is not a topic we like to think about. Again, I think the main reason to do estate planning is not to leave a mess for someone else, typically a family member, to sort out. The best way to approach the subject is to catalogue each asset you have—your home, your IRAs, your bank accounts, etc. If you don't know how they will pass and what the tax consequences will be, I strongly encourage you to talk to your financial advisor or find an estate attorney (your financial advisor or tax preparer can typically provide several referrals to you). I don't think any of us wants our passing to cause problems for our heirs.

Chapter 11 – Charitable Giving

Most of us know that giving to charities typically results in a charitable deduction, subject to limits. I often see charitable giving strategies promoted that are claimed to work even if there is no charitable intent, meaning you come out ahead even if you don't care to give to a charity. It has been my experience that these typically don't bear out. However, for those who do have a charity they would like to support, either during their life or after they pass, there are some very good strategies that can be employed. We will first look at giving during your lifetime.

Lifetime Charitable Giving

Most people have several choices they can make as far as what assets to give to charity. You can give cash, assets such as stocks and bonds, your time, or for those over 70 ½, part or all of your required minimum distribution.

Qualified Charitable Distributions of RMDs

The last item in the list above is one of the most powerful ways, from a tax standpoint, to give to charity. Remember that even if you don't need all the money from your required minimum distribution, you still have to take it out or pay a whopping 50% penalty on the amount you should have taken. For most people excess RMDs result in a form of double taxation; not only are you paying tax on money you don't need, but it is most likely causing more of your Social Security to be taxed.

This strategy is called the IRA Qualified Charitable Distribution (QCD). In years past, QCD had been subject to annual renewal by congress, but at the end of 2015, it became permanent. The QCD allows you to have part, or all, of your RMD paid directly to a qualified charity, up to the annual limit of $100,00. The amount distributed to a charity is <u>excluded</u> from your income. Remember, an exclusion is not added to your adjusted gross income, so it doesn't cause more of your Social Security to be taxable. Without the QCD, if you wanted to give some of your RMD, you would first have to distribute it to yourself, then write a check to your charity. You would typically get a deduction for the charitable gift so the portion of the IRA going to charity wouldn't be taxable, but the amount of your Social Security subject to taxation would still move up. Exclusions are wonderful!

The increase in the standard deduction in 2018 has made the QCD even more relevant now because most people do not contribute enough to charity to exceed the new higher standard deduction.

Gifting Appreciated Assets

It is not uncommon for me to get a call from a client who tells me he wants to support a charity and asks my advice what to sell in order to generate the needed funds. If the client is over 70 ½ I typically discuss the QCD to explore if that is a viable option. If not, I then look at investment accounts, seeking out securities that have a large unrealized gain.

If we sell the security, the client will have the funds he needs, but he will also have to pay capital gains taxes on the sale. Because of the charitable deduction, the gain won't alter his taxes due, other than potentially increasing the amount of Social Security subject to tax. But let's make sure things are even better.

We should give the appreciated security directly to the charity. The client will get the same deduction (fair market value of the security), but he won't have to incur any capital gain taxation. The charity is tax exempt anyway, so it doesn't have to worry about taxes at sale. The security or cash gives the charity the same benefit.

Small charities often do not have a brokerage account. Most advisors would be happy to set up a brokerage account for a charity that can facilitate charitable transactions for them. I did this for a small charity several years ago. After we processed one transaction, the charity mentioned in its newsletter that it was now able to accept donations of appreciated stock. I helped the charity explain how this could benefit its donors, and it saw in turn a nice uptick in donations, essentially a double bonus.

Bruce Larsen

Gifting Very Large Appreciated Assets

Having practiced both in Montana and now in Colorado, I have worked with a lot of farmers and ranchers. In past generations, most farmers and ranchers would pass their holdings down to the next generation. Their retirement would typically be funded by ongoing earnings from the farm or ranch.

Today, we see more and more farmers and ranchers, as well as business owners, approaching retirement with none of their children wanting to continue the family enterprise. This phenomenon, primarily, is driven by the inability of the farm or business to support two generations at the same time so the children moved on to other endeavors.

People in agriculture are finding themselves in a situation where the only way to fund their retirement is by selling the farm or ranch. The same holds for business owners. This typically generates huge capital gains taxes. A couple who inherited a farm from one of their parents 30 years ago with a current value of $3 million would have a cost basis of about $1.3 million, so selling would result in a $1.7 million capital gain. Assuming $120,000 in farm income, this will cause $396,515 in capital gain taxes. If you are good at math, you probably notice that this is over 20% in taxation on the gain—isn't the top capital gains rate 20%? The cause is the new Medicare taxes created by the Affordable Care Act. The effective federal rate on the gain is 23.32%. After paying the taxes, these people have about $2.6 million left to invest to generate income.

While there is no legitimate way to eliminate the taxes due on the sale, there are ways to spread the gain out over a long period of time—typically your lifetime. One of these methods is a *Charitable Remainder Trust* (CRT). This type of trust allows you to donate the asset, such as the farm, to a trust that you control. The trust sells the asset, and you take lifetime distributions from the trust; the charity gets what is left in the trust once you and your spouse have both passed away. This is fairly complicated, so let's walk through an example.

Fred and Debbie Farmer have a farm with the values as listed above. The Farmers have two children, both living out of state with good jobs. Neither of the kids wants to give up a career to come back to the farm to help their parents. Because the farm only generates income, on average, of about $120,000 per year, the place wouldn't support both families anyway.

102

The Farmers are heavily involved with their church and would like to make a meaningful financial contribution at some point. They would also like to be able to leave something for the kids. Ideally, they would like to have the same income they have now. They discuss their financial needs with their financial advisor, Dave. Dave suggests they put in place a charitable remainder trust (CRT).

Several variables drive the operations of a CRT. Dave has access to a calculator that can run the numbers for him. Dave puts in the following variables:

- Dave and Debbie's names and ages (they are both 65)
- Their current tax bracket (15%)
- The value of the farm ($3 million)
- The cost basis of the farm ($1.3 million)
- Current income percentage from farm (4%)
- Trust payout (6%)

Dave's software generates the following illustration:

Fred and Debbie Farmer Charitable Remainder Unitrust	
Value of Donated Assets	3,000,000
Annual Trust Distributions	180,000
Income need	120,000
Excess Distributions	60,000
Excess Distributions Purchase Life Insurance for Children - Benefit	2,800,000
Projected Remainder to Charity	2,872,971
Annual Adjusted Gross Income (taxed as Capital Gain)	180,000
Total Charitable Deduction	817,740
Maximum Annual Deduction Allowed (5 Years)	108,000
Taxable Income	-
Federal Taxes Due	-
Net Income After Tax and After Insurance Premiums	120,000

When the Farmers were operating the farm, their income was the same $120,000, but their federal taxes and both the employee and employer FICA/Medicare taxes were about $27,518 annually. Their net, after tax, was $92,482. The CRT has increased their net after tax, after insurance premiums, to $120,00. This is a fairly good outcome. Keep in mind that the Farmers are most likely eligible for Social Security, increasing their disposable annual income further on they start the benefits. I'm assuming in this example that the trust doesn't earn any ordinary income; it is either capital gain, qualified dividends or tax-exempt income.

The Farmers' tax calculation will change over time. Because of income limitations to charitable contributions, they won't be able to use the entire $817,740 in charitable deduction. They can use $108,000 for the year of the gift as well as carry it forward for the next five years. Year seven, after the deduction is lost, their federal taxes would move up to $2,430 per year, still putting them in a better state than they experienced operating the farm.

If the Farmers wanted to, they could increase the distribution rate. This would result in more income, a smaller deduction, and less money projected to go to the charity. The CRT affords them flexibility to adjust the variables to get the trust in line with what they want to accomplish.

Taxation of a charitable trust is somewhat complicated to keep track of. The donor is taxed based on the character of the income generated by the trust on a *worst in-first-out* basis. This means that if the trust generates ordinary income, it is deemed distributed before any capital gain or qualified dividend. The first transaction of the trust is the capital gain on the sale of the farm. Even if the Farmers invest the proceeds in municipal bonds, and it were possible to get a 6% return on tax free bonds, the Farmers wouldn't have tax-free income distributions until the entire $1.7 million in gain is distributed. This would take about 9.4 years. A preferable strategy would be to invest in qualified dividend stocks and tax free closed-in funds. These should typically provide the income they need without dramatically reducing the amount that will go to charity.

The above paragraph may be TMI (too much information), but I include it because I know of several so-called "Planned Giving" experts who are touting this strategy and claiming the taxable gain does not have to be distributed to the beneficiary. These "experts" claim that you could invest in an immediate annuity and only pay taxes on the amount of the interest distribution, and that the return of principal based on the exclusion ratio is not taxed. The IRS has a longstanding position that gifts to a charity or a trust carry the donor's basis with it; the position was recently affirmed in an IRS notice. Ignoring the gain generated on the sale is going to cause people some serious problems if they are audited.

So far, it would seem this strategy makes a lot of sense for the Farmers. They are taking care of themselves, their kids, and their charity. The analysis wouldn't be complete without comparing what would happen if they sold the farm and invested the money. The chart below reveals their income and tax status if they sold the farm and invested in closed end municipal bond funds; this isn't investment advice - I just want to demonstrate what it looks like at a modest return on investment.

Sell the Farm, Invest the Proceeds	
Value of Farm	3,000,000
Taxes Due on Sale	396,515
Net Proceeds	2,603,485
Gross Income Needed	120,000
Rate of Return Needed on Investments	4.61%
Tax Exempt Income Available (Closed in Municiple Bond Funds)	5.00%
Annual Tax Exempt Income	130,174
Excess Over Need to Charity	10,174
Projected Remainder to Kids	2,603,485

The Farmers have plenty of money to generate the money they need. They can also leave a sizable estate to the children. The charity does not fare quite so well. This is why I mentioned before that this strategy rarely has merit without strong charitable intent; they could generate more income (typically) by paying the taxes and investing the difference.

A word of caution if you decide to employ this strategy—make sure your tax preparer has experience in charitable remainder trust accounting. Over my career, I have taken over investment management of several CRTs. On about half of these, after reviewing the tax filings, I have advised the client to get a new tax preparer because filings were incorrect.

Other Charitable Gifting Strategies

Many charities offer a wide range of charitable gifting options. If you want to gift an appreciated asset to a charity and have lifetime income, but don't want the complications of setting up a CRT, you could instead use a *charitable gift annuity*. You would transfer ownership of the asset to a charity and the annuity would provide a life-time income to you. Anything remaining at the time of your death would then be kept by the charity. A disadvantage in this strategy is that the entire distribution is taxable as ordinary income. You also need to research the charity for credit worthiness to make sure it is financially sound.

A *Charitable Lead Trust* (CLT) works almost opposite to a charitable remainder trust. Like a CRT, you would donate a low cost basis asset. The trust would sell the asset and provide income to the charity (not you) for your lifetime, or joint lifetime of a couple, or a term of years. When you have both passed, the remainder of the trust balance goes to your children. This type of trust works well if you have an asset, say a rental property that you don't need the income from. Remember, even if you don't need the income, you are still taxed on it. If you would be donating the income to charity anyway, the CLT is a much more tax efficient way to do it.

There are several other strategies available to you that are supported by most large charities. Most of these charities have planned-giving staff that can work with you, your financial advisor, and your tax advisor to develop a strategy—or a combination of strategies—that fits your needs.

Conclusion

There are several strategies for charitable gifting available. If you would like to continue to support a charity throughout your retirement, you should discuss this intent with your financial advisor or tax advisor to develop the most tax friendly way to accomplish your goals.

Chapter 12 – Reverse Mortgages

Many people approach the subject of reverse mortgages with skepticism. When reverse mortgages were first created, there were instances of fraud which generated horror stories of seniors being forced out of their homes. The Federal Housing Administration now tightly regulates the industry, and a reverse mortgage can no longer force you or your spouse out of your home, provided you maintain the home, pay real estate taxes, and provide insurance coverage for the home.

What is a Reverse Mortgage?

A reverse mortgage, also called a *Home Equity Conversion Mortgage* (HECM), is a way to convert the equity in your home into tax-free cash without having to make any monthly payments. Instead of monthly payments, the loan is repaid in one lump sum when the last borrower leaves the home.

Many people struggle through retirement never accessing the value of their home equity, which for many is their largest asset. A reverse mortgage can also make sense for those people who are not struggling but want better control over their taxes.

The proceeds you receive from a reverse mortgage, either in the form of a lump sum or monthly/yearly payments, are actually loan advances so they are not included in your income. The cash flow is excluded—which we know is the best form of cash flow. This is the best cash flow you can receive—it does not increase taxation on your Social Security and is tax free.

Many people have a goal of paying the home mortgage off before retiring, sometimes even making extra payments to accomplish this. After the home is paid off, they then have a valuable asset that is giving them no financial benefit. I would encourage you to consider the equity in your home on a level playing field with all other financial assets you own, such as IRAs, savings accounts, and brokerage accounts. Even if you have a goal of leaving your home to your children, you should consider whether accessing the equity in your home allows you to leave more to your children by allowing you to add value in a different way.

When does a reverse mortgage make financial sense? The presenter at a reverse mortgage workshop I attended recently stated that 80% of retirees should consider a reverse mortgage. While this may be an overstatement considering incentives for the presenter, a case for a reverse mortgage is tenable in several instances. Let's take a look at some examples.

Delaying Social Security

Doug and Lisa Jones would like to retire. They are both 65. Their home is valued at $350,000. The Joneses have developed a budget and have determined that they need $5,000 per month to live the lifestyle they would like. If they turn on their Social Security now, they would each receive $1,860 per month. Doug has an IRA worth $250,000, conservatively invested and projected to earn 5% per year.

The "default" retirement plan the Joneses would follow would have them take their Social Security now and make up any difference with future distributions from the IRA. Doug and Lisa also realize that inflation will have to be factored in, which they assume will average 2.6% over the span of their retirement years. They will use this factor to increase both their living expenses and their Social Security benefits.

If they were to develop a spreadsheet of their retirement cash flow, it would look like the one on the following page.

			Doug and Lisa Jones Income Plan				
Age	Social Security	IRA Dist	Gross Income	Federal Taxes	Net Income	Income Need	Shortfall
65	44,640	15,360	60,000	-	60,000	60,000	-
66	45,801	15,759	61,560	-	61,560	61,560	-
67	46,990	16,171	63,161	-	63,161	63,161	-
68	48,212	16,591	64,803	-	64,803	64,803	-
69	49,466	17,022	66,488	-	66,488	66,488	-
70	50,752	17,464	68,216	-	68,216	68,216	-
71	52,072	17,918	69,990	-	69,990	69,990	-
72	53,426	18,384	71,810	-	71,810	71,810	-
73	54,816	18,861	73,677	-	73,677	73,677	-
74	56,242	19,350	75,592	-	75,592	75,592	-
75	57,704	19,853	77,558	-	77,558	77,558	-
76	59,205	20,371	79,575	1	79,574	79,574	-
77	60,744	21,081	81,825	182	81,643	81,643	-
78	62,323	21,731	84,054	288	83,766	83,766	-
79	63,944	22,397	86,341	397	85,944	85,944	-
80	65,606	23,084	88,690	512	88,178	88,178	-
81	67,312	23,792	91,104	633	90,471	90,471	-
82	69,062	24,512	93,574	751	92,823	92,823	-
83	70,858	25,263	96,121	884	95,237	95,237	-
84	72,700	26,019	98,719	1,006	97,713	97,713	-
85	74,590	2,329	76,919		76,919	100,253	23,334
86	76,530		76,530		76,530	102,860	26,330
87	78,519		78,519		78,519	105,534	27,015
88	80,561		80,561		80,561	108,278	27,717
89	82,655		82,655		82,655	111,093	28,438
90	84,804		84,804		84,804	113,982	29,177
91	87,009		87,009		87,009	116,945	29,936
92	89,272		89,272		89,272	119,986	30,714

They recognize that they have a problem if they live past age 84. They will deplete the balance of Doug's IRA at that age and will have only Social Security to live on. They know that they have the home fully paid for so they reason that they could pull money out of the home in a home equity line, but they are concerned that the bank may not lend to them since their only income would be Social Security. They also realize, as of 2018, the interest on home equity loans is no longer deductible unless used for home improvement.

The Joneses take another look at their Social Security statement and see that if they delay their benefits until 70, they will have $63,360 in benefits ($71,686 adjusted for COLA of 2.5%). They take another stab at their spreadsheet, this time using the IRA to get them to age 70. The resultant spreadsheet is shown below.

| | Doug and Lisa Jones Income Plan | | | | | | |
| | Delay Social Security | | | | | | |
Age	Social Security	IRA Dist	Gross Income	Federal Taxes	Net Income	Income Need	Excess (Shortfall)
65	-	64,835	64,835	4,835	60,000	60,000	-
66	-	65,794	65,794	4,234	61,560	61,560	-
67	-	67,533	67,533	4,372	63,161	63,161	-
68	-	69,291	69,291	4,488	64,803	64,803	-
69	-	12,258	12,258	-	12,258	66,488	(54,230)
70	71,586	-	71,586	-	71,586	68,216	3,370
71	73,376	-	73,376	-	73,376	69,990	3,386
72	75,210	-	75,210	-	75,210	71,810	3,400
73	77,090	-	77,090	-	77,090	73,677	3,414
74	79,018	-	79,018	-	79,018	75,592	3,425
75	80,993	-	80,993	-	80,993	77,558	3,435
76	83,018	-	83,018	-	83,018	79,574	3,444
77	85,093	-	85,093	-	85,093	81,643	3,450
78	87,221	-	87,221	-	87,221	83,766	3,455
79	89,401	-	89,401	-	89,401	85,944	3,457
80	91,636	-	91,636	-	91,636	88,178	3,458
81	93,927	-	93,927	-	93,927	90,471	3,456
82	96,275	-	96,275	-	96,275	92,823	3,452
83	98,682	-	98,682	-	98,682	95,237	3,446
84	101,149	-	101,149	-	101,149	97,713	3,436
85	103,678	-	103,678	-	103,678	100,253	3,425
86	106,270	-	106,270	-	106,270	102,860	3,410
87	108,927	-	108,927	-	108,927	105,534	3,392
88	111,650	-	111,650	-	111,650	108,278	3,372
89	114,441	-	114,441	-	114,441	111,093	3,348
90	117,302	-	117,302	-	117,302	113,982	3,320
91	120,235	-	120,235	-	120,235	116,945	3,289
92	123,240	-	123,240	-	123,240	119,986	3,255

This strategy isn't working out too well either. The IRA balance plus earnings will not get them to age 70. They could turn on their Social Security when the IRA depletes, but that wouldn't give them enough to live on for the rest of their lives. Again, they could take out a home equity line and pay it off with excess earnings going forward.

The Joneses consider other alternatives, such as working for another year or trying to live on a little less. None of the alternatives sounds that good to them. They decide to visit with a financial advisor, Katie Smith, to see if she can come up with a plan they haven't considered. She suggests that they consider a reverse mortgage. Doug and Lisa aren't wild about the idea because they had planned to leave the home to their children. Lisa asks Katie to demonstrate how the reverse mortgage strategy might affect their legacy for the kids. Katie responds, "Give me time. I'll have to work that out." The Joneses assent, and the three set a time the following week to get together.

Katie develops the following spreadsheet.

| | | | | Doug and Lisa Jones Income Plan | | | | |
| | | | | Delay Social Security - Use Reverse Mortgage | | | | |
Age	Social Security	IRA Dist	Reverse Mortgage	Gross Cash Flow	Federal Taxes	Net Income	Income Need	Excess (Shortfall)
65	-	30,818	30,000	60,818	818	60,000	60,000	-
66	-	31,163	30,780	61,943	383	61,560	61,560	-
67	-	32,002	31,580	63,582	421	63,161	63,161	-
68	-	32,835	32,401	65,236	433	64,803	64,803	-
69	-	33,705	33,243	66,948	460	66,488	66,488	-
70	71,586	5,004	-	76,590	-	76,590	68,216	8,374
71	73,376	5,244	-	78,620	-	78,620	69,990	8,630
72	75,210	6,494	-	81,704	-	81,704	71,810	9,894
73	77,090	5,757	-	82,847	-	82,847	73,677	9,171
74	79,018	6,031	-	85,049	-	85,049	75,592	9,456
75	80,993	6,319	-	87,312	-	87,312	77,558	9,754
76	83,018	6,619	-	89,637	-	89,637	79,574	10,063
77	85,093	6,900	-	91,993	-	91,993	81,643	10,350
78	87,221	7,226	-	94,447	-	94,447	83,766	10,681
79	89,401	7,528	-	96,929	-	96,929	85,944	10,985
80	91,636	7,840	-	99,476	-	99,476	88,178	11,298
81	93,927	8,162	-	102,089	-	102,089	90,471	11,618
82	96,275	8,494	-	104,769	-	104,769	92,823	11,946
83	98,682	8,835	-	107,517	-	107,517	95,237	12,281
84	101,149	9,185	-	110,334	-	110,334	97,713	12,621
85	103,678	9,480	-	113,158	-	113,158	100,253	12,905
86	106,270	9,776	-	116,046	-	116,046	102,860	13,186
87	108,927	10,071	-	118,998	-	118,998	105,534	13,463
88	111,650	10,365	-	122,015	-	122,015	108,278	13,737
89	114,441	10,654	-	125,095	-	125,095	111,093	14,002
90	117,302	10,841	-	128,143	-	128,143	113,982	14,161
91	120,235	11,012	-	131,247	-	131,247	116,945	14,301
92	123,240	11,163	-	134,403	-	134,403	119,986	14,418

By using the reverse mortgage to get the Joneses to age 70, they have to take out much less from Doug's IRA, which also means they pay less tax. At age 70, the IRA will be down to about $145,000. If they only take out the RMDs until 92, and the IRA continues to earn 5%, the balance at age 92 will be about $108,395. If they invest their excess earnings each year at 3.08% tax-exempt, they will have an additional account balance to leave the kids about $406,420. The total of the IRA plus the excess account is $515,275. In addition to this, there would still be a little equity left in the house. Katie asks the couple if this is enough to leave to the kids. The Joneses think it over and decide the IRA is sufficient legacy, and they decide they will use the excess earnings each year to take a nice trip, rather than invest in tax-exempt securities.

One of the nice things about using the reverse mortgage is that mortgagees don't have to pay any taxes on the money they access via the reverse mortgage. This allows them to reduce their tax bill significantly compared to taking all the needed funds from their IRA.

A reverse mortgage can also be set up to pay long-term care premiums. I had some clients ask me to get long term care quotes for them. The quotes came in at about $8,500 per year combined. The problem was that the only means accessible for funding the premiums were their IRAs. Taking an additional $8,500 out of their IRAs increased their taxes by about $4,000 due to the distribution, as well as an increased level of Social Security taxation. When you add the $4,000 of taxes to the premium, their net out of pocket is $12,500. This made the policies unaffordable.

The reverse mortgage we have looked at for the Joneses could be structured to provide lifetime income payments. In their situation, this would be about $11,100 annually. For people who are very concerned about the possibility of needing extended long-term care, a reverse mortgage can be a tax free way of funding the premiums.

People with No Legacy Goals

For some people nearing retirement, who have successful kids, legacy is not a primary concern. Many retirees reason that they paid to raise the kids and get them through college; now they want to enjoy their remaining years as much as possible.

While it is traditional to leave the family home to our children, I would encourage you to ask your children which they would prefer: getting a paid-for home after you both die, or seeing you enjoy yourselves as much as possible in your later years. If my kids told me they would want the home, I'd go ahead and disinherit them anyway, removing any need for legacy assets (not really, but I'd strongly consider it!).

A couple at age 70 with a $400,000 home value could generate an additional monthly tax-free cash flow from a reverse mortgage of about $1,200 per month ($14,400 annually). This could make a huge difference in most people's quality of life.

Conclusion

Don't just consider a reverse mortgage as a last resort option. The equity in your home is an asset. It shouldn't be viewed only as something to be passed on to the kids. Modern reverse mortgages are very flexible, allowing their use for a wide range of financial goals.

Chapter 13 – A Tax-Free Retirement

The goal of paying no taxes in retirement typically doesn't get reached. Nor should it. Structuring assets so that no taxes are due, very likely puts you in a less desirable financial position over time than if you pay some taxes along the way. Yet, a no-tax retirement is possible.

Two years ago, I met with a man, Dave, from Wyoming (a state with no state income taxes). Dave was an engineer who was retiring. He had never been married and was completely debt free. Dave had earned over $200,000 inflation-adjusted throughout his career and, especially since he was single, had paid a lot of taxes along the way.

Dave said he was very comfortable living on $60,000 per year. He was adamant that he never wanted to pay taxes again. I explained to him that there was no way to accomplish his goal but, if he wanted to pay a lot in tax the first year, we could get him to a tax-free status for the remainder of his retirement. I also explained that this would probably result in more total lifetime taxes than if we were to opt for a more traditional plan with a steady, nominal annual tax burden. He asked to see both work-ups side by side.

I catalogued Dave's assets and looked at his Social Security benefits. His plan variables are summarized on the next page:

Dave's Current Situation	
Dave's Age	66
Dave's Social Security at 66	32,400
Dave's Social Security at 70	42,768
Dave's Roth IRA (Rate of Return 7%)	120,000
Dave's Traditional IRA (Rate of Return 7%)	200,000
Dave's Taxable Savings (Rate of Return 1% Taxable)	600,000
Income Need	60,000

	Dave's Current Tax Situation					
Age	Income Need	Social Security	Dist from Savings	Dist from IRA	Taxable Interest	Taxes Due
66	60,000	-	55,650	4,350	6,000	-
67	61,560	-	56,444	5,116	5,504	-
68	63,161	-	57,259	5,901	4,994	-
69	64,803	-	58,096	6,707	4,471	-
70	66,488	47,577	18,911	-	3,935	-
71	68,216	48,862	770	9,292	3,785	879

I pointed out to Dave that $879 in taxes on $68,216 in income wasn't a lot to be paying. Having read the previous chapters of this book, Dave replied, "Yeah, that plays out this time frame, but how will it play down the road as my Social Security and required minimum distributions increase?"

I told Dave that converting all of his IRA to a Roth IRA and investing his taxable savings in a conservative municipal bond portfolio yielding about 2.5% could avert the predicament he had posed. Dave told me to devise a table that projected what that would look like. Dave's projected tax status under the stratagem I proposed appears in the table on the next page.

	Dave's Tax Free Situation					
Age	Income Need	Social Security	Dist from M Bonds	Dist from Roth	Taxable Interest	Taxes Due
66	60,000	-	106,138	-	-	46,138
67	61,560	-	61,560	-	-	-
68	63,161	-	63,161	-	-	-
69	64,803	-	64,803	-	-	-
70	66,488	47,577	10,056	8,855	-	-
71	68,216	48,862	10,056	9,299	-	-

Dave asked me if this plan would insure that he would never have to pay taxes again. I reminded him that the limits set for the taxation of Social Security are not indexed for inflation. Inflation ultimately determines tax obligation. I couldn't guarantee zero tax. Dave told me to tweak the plan in order to get rid of municipal bond interest that could cause tax on more of his Social Security in the future. We discussed options and settled on a plan for Dave at age 71 that put the remaining balance of the bond account into a deferred annuity. The result appears in the following chart:

	Dave's Tax Free Situation - Annuity					
Age	Income Need	Social Security	Dist from M Bonds	Dist from Roth	Taxable Interest	Taxes Due
66	60,000	-	106,138	-	-	46,138
67	61,560	-	61,560	-	-	-
68	63,161	-	63,161	-	-	-
69	64,803	-	64,803	-	-	-
70	66,488	47,577	10,056	8,855	-	-
71	68,216	48,862	-	19,355	-	-

I pointed out to Dave that the Roth distribution represented a distribution rate of 4% that should be sustainable if he continued to get his expected return of 7%.

Dave was happy with the outcome. He did ask me, however, if I could be absolutely sure he would never pay taxes after the first year. I told him that based on current law I could, but that there was no way to absolutely predict what Congress may do in the future. There are proposals floating around to change how Social Security is taxed, based on other assets and earnings. Of course, as long as we have politicians there will always be uncertainty, but this was as close as we could get.

Conclusion

While for most people it is possible to get to a tax-free retirement, the cost in net to get there almost always exceeds the lifetime taxes that would be due following a traditional, tax-smart strategy. Taxes will most likely continue to be a moving target. Retirement plans should be updated on an annual basis to get an accurate estimate of taxes as the tax landscape changes over time.

Chapter 14 – Tax Reference

This chapter will provide a reference for the most commonly used tax tables. Beneath each table, I will present a review of several pertinent key concepts, as well as an index of treatment of these concepts throughout the book's previous chapters.

Deductions and Personal Exemptions

The examples in this book use the standard deduction, which is what most retirees in the $60,000 to $160,000 in net after tax income find most advantageous (the chief exception would be retirees still paying on a mortgage when they enter retirement, or who have other large deductions). The standard deductions and exemptions are shown below:

Standard Deduction and Personal Exemptions	
Standard Deductions	
Married/Filing jointly and qualfying widow(er)s	24,000
Single	12,000
Extra Amount per person if blind or over age 65	1,300
Personal Exemptions* - per person	-
* Personal exemptions and itemized deductions phase out beginning with AGI over $259,400 (single) or $311,300 (married/ filing jointly and qualifying widow(er)s if 2018 act sunsets.	

For those reading this book and still working, you will probably have more deductions than those in retirement. Retirees typically do not have enough deductions to itemize unless they have significant health care expenses. If you are able to itemize deductions, you should be aware that recent tax law changes have changed the limitations of several deductions. The following table outlines the most common itemized deductions and whether they are subject to the phase-out limits in the proceeding chart.

Deductions not Subject to Phase Out
Medical and dental expenses in exess of 7.5% (2018) 10% (after)
Investment interest expenses
Casualty and theft losses in Federally Declared Areas
Casualty and theft losses from income-producing property
Gambling losses
Deductions Subject to Phase Out
Home mortgage interest for mortgage amount under $750,000
State and Local Taxes up to $10,000
Gifts to charity - not currently subject to phase out.
~~Job expenses and certain miscellaneous dedcutions~~
~~Other miscellaneous deductions~~

I realize this is confusing. The 2018 tax law removes most phase-outs, but entirely eliminates miscellaneous deductions subject to the 2% AGI flow. I left them in the chart because if the new law isn't re-authorized it will sunset in 2025 and we will go back to old tax law.

I have always found it interesting that gambling losses are not subject to phase out. I can only conclude from this that members of Congress must spend a lot of their time gambling—and losing—and want to make sure they can take advantage of deducting their losses.

Retirement Plan Contributions

Limits on the allowable pre-tax amounts of deductible contributions into your retirement plan at work appear on the chart on the next page. Phase out of deductions does not come into play. Contributions to retirement plans are excluded from your adjusted gross income, but they are included in the amount of your wages subject to Social Security.

The amount of your share of the health insurance premium you pay on your company sponsored group plan is also excluded. Once you retire, any medical expenses you would like to deduct, including health insurance premiums, are limited to expenses that exceed 10% of AGI (7.5% if you are 65 or over). This is one of the few instances where you are worse off, from a tax standpoint, once you retire. Getting back to retirement plan contributions, the limits are shown below:

Contribution Limits to Employer Sponsored Plans	
Maximum elective deferral for 401(k), 403(b) plans, under 50 years old	18,500
Maximum elective deferral for 401(k), 402(b) plans, 50 years and older	24,500
Maximum elective deferral for SIMPLE IRA plans, under 50 years old	12,500
Maximum elective deferral for SIMPLE IRA plans, 50 years and older	15,500
Maximum elective deferral to 457 plans of gov't and tax-exempt employers	18,500
Limit on annual additions to defined contribution plans (employee and employer)	55,000
Annual compensation threshold requiring SEP contributions	600
Limit on annual additions to SEP plans	55,000
Maximum annual compensation taken into account for contributions	270,000
Annual benefit limit under defined benefit plans (pensions)	215,000
Limitation used in definition of highly compensated employee	120,000
Health flexible spending account maximum salary reduction contribution	3,450

Traditional and Roth Contributions

Whether you can contribute to a traditional IRA or a Roth IRA depends both on your participation in a employer-sponsored plan and your income. See the table on the next page:

Traditional IRA Deductions			
Filing Status	Covered by employer's retirement plan?	2018 Modified AGI	Deductibility
Single	No	Any amount	Full
	Yes	$63,000 or less	Full
	Yes	$63,000 - $72,999	Partial
	Yes	$73,000 or more	None
Married/ Jointly	Neither spouse covered	Any amount	Full
Married/ Jointly	Both spouses covered	$101,000 or less	Full
		$101,001 - $120,999	Partial
		$121,000 or more	None
Married/ Jointly	Yes, but spouse is not covered	$101,000 or less	Full
		$101,001 - $120,999	Partial
		$121,000 or more	None
Married/ Jointly	No, but spouse is covered	$189,000 or less	Full
		$189,001 - $199,999	Partial
		$199,000 or more	None

The chart above shows the eligibility to make a deductible contribution to a traditional IRA. You can make a non-deductible contribution regardless of income level, provided you are under 70 ½.

Your ability to contribute to a Roth IRA is restricted as shown below.

Roth IRA's		
Maximum annual contributions		
Under age 50, lessor of earned income or $5,500		
Age 50 and over, lessor of earned income or $6,500		
Contribution eligibility		
Filing Status	2016 Modified AGI	Contribution?
Single	Less than $120,000	Full Contribution
	$120,001 - $135,000	Partial Contribution
Married/ Jointly	Less than $189,000	Full Contribution
	$189,001 - $199,000	Partial Contribution

The contribution to Roth IRAs is the same as for traditional IRAs.

Above I mentioned that you can always contribute to an IRA, although participation in employer-sponsored plans and income limits determine if the contribution is deductible. Why would anyone want to make a non-deductible contribution to a traditional IRA? Remember in Chapter 5 I noted that anyone can convert a traditional IRA to a Roth IRA. You could make a non-deductible contribution to a traditional IRA and then, the following year you could convert the traditional IRA to a Roth IRA. Because there are no gains in the traditional IRA (assuming you left it in cash) and because the money is after-tax, no taxes would be due on the conversion.

The above strategy only works if you have no other IRAs. If there are other IRA balances in other accounts, the conversion is subject to the pro rata rules of the IRS that say all IRAs are assumed to be one IRA and the amount converted would be partial after-tax and partial before-tax contributions. If this is the case, you could roll all of your IRA balances into your 401(k) prior to starting this strategy.

Federal Income Tax Brackets and Rates

Once you have determined how much your adjusted gross income is, including the taxable portion of your Social Security, you reduce this amount by either your itemized deductions or standard deduction along with a further reduction by your personal exemptions (if not phased out). This gives you your taxable income.

Taxable income is then taxed by amount range and by the characterization of the income, either ordinary income or capital gains. Tax on ordinary income appears in the following table:

Ordinary Income Tax			
Filing Status	If taxable income is over	but not over	Tax Rate
Married/Filing jointly and qualifying widow(er)s	-	19,050	10%
	19,050	77,400	12%
	77,400	165,000	22%
	165,000	315,000	24%
	315,000	400,000	32%
	400,000	600,000	35%
	600,000	-	37%
Single	-	9,525	10%
	9,525	38,700	12%
	38,700	82,500	22%
	82,500	157,500	24%
	157,500	200,000	32%
	200,000	500,000	35%
	500,000	-	37%
Estate and Trusts	-	2,550	10%
	2,550	9,150	24%
	9,150	1,250	35%
	1,250		37%

Long term capital gain and ordinary income are taxed based on the tax bracket you fall into. The bracket is determined based on AGI, which includes the capital gain and/or qualified dividends. The tax rates are shown below, along with an explanation of the net investment income tax.

Tax on Capital Gains and Qualfied Dividends	
Tax Bracket	Long-term (> 12 months) capital gains and qualified dividends
10% and 12% brackets	0%
2% through 35% brackets	15%
37% bracket	20%
Additional 3.8% federal net investment income (NII) tax applies to indiviudals on the less of NII or modified AGI in excess of $200,000 (single) or $250,000 (married/filing jointly and qualifying widow(er)s. Also applies to any trust or estate on the lessor of undistributed net income or AGI in excess of the dollar amount at which the estate/trust pays income taxes at the highest rate	

Estate Taxes

I have mentioned previously that generally the readers that this book targets rarely have to pay estate taxes. The gross estate exemption is $5,450.00. Estates of some exceed the exemption. I include estate tax information, shown below:

Death/Gifts Occuring in 2018*		
If gift/gross estae is		Tax
over	but not over	Rate
-	10,000	18%
10,000	20,000	20%
20,000	40,000	22%
40,000	60,000	24%
60,000	80,000	26%
80,000	100,000	28%
100,000	150,000	30%
150,000	250,000	32%
250,000	500,000	34%
500,000	750,000	37%
750,000	1,000,000	39%
1,000,000	-	40%
* Annual gift tax exclusion (2018): Individual, $15,000; Married electing split gifts, $30,000. Combined lifetime gift tax and gross estate tax exemptions: $11,180,000 GST tax exemption: $11,180,000.		

For most of my clients, estate taxes aren't an issue. Gifting is more often an issue. Many people make and receive gifts larger than $15,000 per year. If a gift is made that exceeds the gift tax exclusion, no taxes are typically due. Nevertheless, a gift tax return is required to be filed by the person making the gift. The amount of the gift over the exclusion amount reduces in turn the recipient's estate tax exemption.

Miscellaneous Tax Information

Expressly, it has not been my intention to parse the entire U.S. tax code. The following is information salient to the most common issues that my clients face.

Social Security

I have previously covered provisional income, which determines the point that a portion of your Social Security benefits become taxable. Another point to keep in mind, especially if you decide to file prior to full retirement age, is reduction in benefits if you continue to work.

If you file for benefits prior to full retirement age (FRA), your benefits reduce by $1 for every $2 you earn over $17,040. The year you reach full retirement age, the limit increases to $45,360 and your benefit reduces by $1 for every $3 over the limit. The $45,360 amount is prorated monthly up until your full retirement birthday; at that point, there is no reduction in benefits.

The earnings limits only apply to W-2 or self-employment earnings. You can make as much as you want from interest, IRA distributions, etc., with no reduction in benefits.

FICA/Medicare Taxes

While working, the amount of your compensation subject to OASDI (Social Security tax) is $128,700; the 6.2%. Medicare taxes (1.45%) used to have similar limits as OASDI, but it not has no cap. If you are self-employed you pay double these rates.

An additional tax of 1.8% applies to people earning over $200,000 (single) and $250,000 (joint). The additional tax is on the excess over these limits.

American Opportunity Tax Credit

Modified AGI Phaseouts for American Opportunity Credit	
Married/Filing Jointly	$160,001 - $179,999
Others	$80,001 - $89,999

Lifetime Learning Credit

Modified AGI Phaseouts for Lifetime Learning Credit	
Married/Filing Jointly	$111,001 - $130,999
Others	$55,001 - $64,999

U.S. Savings Bond Income Used for Higher Education Expenses

Modified AGI Phaseouts for Exclusion of U.S. Savings Bond Income Used for Higher Education Expenses	
Married/Filing Jointly	$116,301 - $146,299
Others	$77,551 - $92,549

Contributions to Coverdell Education Savings Accounts

Modified AGI Phaseouts for Contributions to Coverdell Education Savings Accounts - Maximum contribution is $2,000 per Beneficiary, per Year	
Married/Filing Jointly	$190,001 - $219,999
Others	$95,001 - $109,999

Alternative Minimum Tax

2018 AMT Exemptions	
Filing Status	Exemption
Married/Filing Jointly	109,400
Single	70,300
Phases out beginning with the alternative minimum taxable income over $500,000 (single) or $1 mil. (married/filing jointly and qualifying widow(er)s or $1 mil. (estates and trusts).	

Conclusion

The last few tables should make it clear how complex the tax code is. Everything above refers only to federal taxes. The next chapter will cover the main points of state income tax to keep in mind.

When it comes to tax planning, I strongly urge you not to be a "do-it-yourselfer." Tax codes apply for individual taxpayers disparately and, more often than not, counter-intuitively. Spread over an entire retirement life, very small mistakes or the most innocent of oversights can produce catastrophic impacts. Put a trusted retirement tax team in place.

I'm reminded of a conversation I once had with an Ear, Nose and Throat surgeon. I asked him whom he used for his financial planning, and he told me that with all the information he could access on the internet he could do everything himself and save a few bucks. I told him that when my son needed his tonsils taken out, I probably could have gone on the internet and figured out how to do it myself, but thought it might be better to use someone like him who had done it a few times. After giving it some thought for a few days, the surgeon made an appointment for me to give him a second opinion on what he had going on. While I couldn't fault his investment philosophy, it turned out that details of his tax strategy made no sense at all.

We all have our areas of expertise. Unless you want to start a second career learning all you can about the 77,000 pages of the U.S. Tax Code, I urge you to find a competent financial or tax professional to be your guide on your retirement journey.

Chapter 15 – State Income Taxes

The calculation of state income taxes due in some states is nearly as complicated as the federal return. This chapter does not cover the intricacies of each state's tax policy. Instead, it will focus on the tax issues most often encountered by my middle income retired clients.

I will cover each state individually. Along with state income taxes, I will also mention property tax relief available to seniors in most states.

Alabama

Social security, military, civil service, state and local government pension income and qualified private pensions are exempt from state income tax. Your federal taxes paid can also be deducted if you itemize.

Alabama has three tax brackets. The brackets do not index for inflation.

Alabama Tax Brackets					
Single			Joint		
From	To	Rate	From	To	Rate
-	500	2.00%	-	1,000	2.00%
500	3,000	4.00%	1,000	6,000	4.00%
3,000 +		5.00%	6,000 +	2,000 +	5.00%
Standard Deduction Single		2,500			
Standard Deduction Joint		7,500			
Personal Exemption Single		1,500			
Personal Exemption Joint		3,000			
Additional Personal Exemptions		1,000			

Homeowners age 65 and older are exempt from all state property taxes.

Alaska

Alaska has no income tax. Homeowners age 65 and older (or a surviving spouse 60 and older) are exempt from municipal taxes on the first $150,000 of the assessed value of their property in municipalities that assess property taxes. The exemption also applies to disabled veterans.

Arizona

Social Security and railroad retirement benefits are exempt from Arizona state income taxes. Up to $2,500 of military, civil service, and Arizona state/local pensions are also exempt. All taxes income from all out-of-state government pensions. Arizona does not allow a deduction for federal taxes paid.

The following table outlines the state income tax brackets in Arizona. They do not index for inflation.

Arizona Tax Brackets					
Single			Joint		
From	To	Rate	From	To	Rate
-	10,179	2.59%	-	20,357	2.59%
10,179	25,445	2.88%	20,357	50,890	2.88%
25,445	50,890	3.36%	50,890	101,779	3.36%
50,890	152,668	4.24%	101,779	305,336	4.24%
150,000 +		4.54%	300,000 +		4.54%
Standard Deduction Single	2,099				
Standard Deduction Joint	10,189				
Personal Exemption Single	2,100				
Personal Exemption Joint	4,200				
Additional Personal Exemptions	2,100				

Arizona does offer some property tax relief to seniors, but there is considerable variation across taxing authorities. The state has no property tax; municipalities or counties levy property taxes.

Arkansas

Social Security and railroad retirement benefits are exempt from state income taxes. Up to $6,000 in military, civil service, state and local government, and private pensions are also exempt. IRA distributions can be included as part of the pension exemption.

Arkansas Tax Brackets					
Single			Joint		
From	To	Rate	From	To	Rate
-	4,299	0.90%	-	4,299	0.90%
4,299	8,500	2.50%	4,299	8,500	2.50%
8,500	12,699	3.50%	8,500	12,699	3.50%
12,699	21,199	4.50%	12,699	21,199	4.50%
21,199	35,100	6.00%	21,199	35,100	6.00%
35,100	+	6.90%	35,100	+	6.90%
Standard Deduction Single	2,200				
Standard Deduction Joint	4,400				
Personal Exemption Single	26				
Personal Exemption Joint	52				
Additional Personal Exemptio	26				

Arkansas has relatively small personal exemptions but you can take a double exemption if you are 65 or older.

California

Social Security and railroad retirement benefits are exempt from state income taxes. California taxes private, federal, state and local pensions. Along with the highest state tax rates, California has relatively low standard deductions and personal exemptions.

California Tax Brackets					
Single			Joint		
From	To	Rate	From	To	Rate
-	8,015	1.00%	-	16,030	1.00%
8,015	19,001	2.00%	16,030	38,002	2.00%
19,001	29,989	4.00%	38,002	59,978	4.00%
29,989	41,629	6.00%	59,978	83,258	6.00%
41,629	52,612	8.00%	83,258	105,224	8.00%
52,612	268,750	9.30%	105,224	537,500	9.30%
268,750	322,499	10.30%	537,500	644,988	10.30%
322,499	537,498	11.30%	644,988	1,000,000	11.30%
537,498	1,000,000	12.30%	1,000,000	1,074,996	12.30%
1,000,000	+	13.30%	1,074,996	+	13.30%
Standard Deduction Single		4,236			
Standard Deduction Joint		8,472			
Personal Exemption Single		114			
Personal Exemption Joint		228			
Additional Personal Exemptions		353			

Prior to 2008/2009, some relief for seniors on real estate taxes had been available; this program has been discontinued.

Colorado

Colorado allows those age 55 to 64 to exclude up to $20,000 in pension income. The exclusion increases to $24,000 for those over age 65. The definition of pension is very broad; it includes not only all pension income, but also the taxable portion of your Social Security and distributions from retirement accounts.

Colorado has a flat rate of 4.63% based generally on federal taxable income less the pension exclusion.

A homestead exemption is available to seniors who are 65 or older and have owned and lived in their home for at least 10 years. For those who qualify, up to 50% of their home value (up to a maximum reduction of $200,000) is excluded from property taxes. Renters in the same age group can receive a rebate of up to $600 of the property tax on their residence and $192 of their heating expenses paid during the year, either paid directly or paid as part of their rent.

Connecticut

Connecticut exempts military pensions from state taxation. Social Security benefits are also exempt if your federal adjusted gross income is less than $50,000 single, $60,000 for joint filers.

Connecticut Tax Brackets					
Single			Joint		
From	To	Rate	From	To	Rate
-	10,000	3.00%	-	20,000	3.00%
10,000	50,000	5.00%	20,000	100,000	5.00%
50,000	100,000	5.50%	100,000	200,000	5.50%
100,000	200,000	6.00%	200,000	400,000	6.00%
200,000	250,000	6.50%	400,000	500,000	6.50%
250,000	500,000	6.90%	500,000	1,000,000	6.90%
500,000	+	6.99%	1,000,000	+	6.99%
Standard Deduction Single	-				
Standard Deduction Joint	-				
Personal Exemption Single	15,000	as a credit			
Personal Exemption Joint	-				
Additional Personal Exemptions	-				

A tax credit or rent rebate may be available to residents; income parameters apply.

Delaware

Delaware exempts Social Security and railroad retirement benefits. Up to $12,500 of investment and qualified pension income are also exempt. An exclusion of $2,000 for military pensions is available at any age; the exclusion increases to $12,500 at age 60.

The standard deduction is doubled for filers age 65 and older, who do not itemize.

Delaware Tax Brackets					
Single			Joint		
From	To	Rate	From	To	Rate
-	2,000	0.00%	-	2,000	0.00%
2,000	5,000	2.20%	2,000	5,000	2.20%
5,000	10,000	3.90%	5,000	10,000	3.90%
10,000	20,000	4.80%	10,000	20,000	4.80%
20,000	25,000	5.20%	20,000	25,000	5.20%
25,000	60,000	5.55%	25,000	60,000	5.55%
60,000	+	6.60%	60,000	+	6.60%
Standard Deduction Single	3,250				
Standard Deduction Joint	6,500				
Personal Exemption Single	110				
Personal Exemption Joint	220				
Additional Personal Exemptions	110				

A credit equal to half of a home owner's school property tax is available for those 65 and older.

District of Columbia

Social Security income is exempt. Taxpayers 62 and older can exclude up to $3,000 of military, federal, and local pension. State government pensions are fully taxed.

District of Columbia Tax Brackets					
Single			Joint		
From	To	Rate	From	To	Rate
-	10,000	4.00%	-	10,000	4.00%
10,000	40,000	6.00%	10,000	40,000	6.00%
40,000	60,000	6.50%	40,000	60,000	6.50%
60,000	350,000	8.50%	60,000	350,000	8.50%
350,000	1,000,000	8.75%	350,000	1,000,000	8.75%
1,000,000	+	8.95%	1,000,000	+	8.95%
Standard Deduction Single		5,650			
Standard Deduction Joint		10,275			
Personal Exemption Single		1,775			
Personal Exemption Joint		3,550			
Additional Personal Exemptions		1,775			

The first $67,500 of value is excluded from personal residence property tax. The exemption is increased by $33,750 for homeowners 65 and older with adjusted gross income under $100,000.

Florida

Florida has no state income tax.

Homestead exemptions are available on personal real estate of up to $50,000 of value. The first $25,000 applies to all property taxes, including school district taxes. The second $25,000 applies to the assessed value between $50,000 and $75,000 and only to non-school taxes. An additional exemption is available for homeowners over age 65.

Georgia

Social Security is exempt from state income taxes. A retirement adjustment, that is too complicated to explain here, is available for tax payers over 62.

Georgia Tax Brackets					
Single			Joint		
From	To	Rate	From	To	Rate
-	750	1.00%	-	1,000	1.00%
750	2,250	2.00%	1,000	3,000	2.00%
2,250	3,750	3.00%	3,000	5,000	3.00%
3,750	5,250	4.00%	5,000	7,000	4.00%
5,250	7,000	5.00%	7,000	10,000	5.00%
7,000	+	6.00%	10,000	+	6.00%
Standard Deduction Single	2,300				
Standard Deduction Joint	3,000				
Personal Exemption Single	2,700				
Personal Exemption Joint	5,400				
Additional Personal Exemptions	3,000				

Georgia allows you to double your personal exemption at age 65.

Property is taxed at the county, city, school or state depending on location. Some senior property tax relief is available, especially for lower earners, but it is too complex to detail here.

Hawaii

Social Security, first tier railroad retirement benefits, military, federal, state/local, and the employer portion of private pensions are exempt.

Hawaii Tax Brackets					
Single			Joint		
From	To	Rate	From	To	Rate
-	2,400	1.40%	-	4,800	1.40%
2,400	4,800	3.20%	4,800	9,600	3.20%
4,800	9,600	5.50%	9,600	19,200	5.50%
9,600	14,400	6.40%	19,200	28,800	6.40%
14,400	19,200	6.80%	28,800	38,400	6.80%
19,200	24,000	7.20%	38,400	48,000	7.20%
24,000	36,000	7.60%	48,000	72,000	7.60%
36,000	48,000	7.90%	72,000	96,000	7.90%
48,000	+	8.25%	96,000	+	8.25%
Standard Deduction Single	2,200				
Standard Deduction Joint	4,400				
Personal Exemption Single	1,144				
Personal Exemption Joint	2,288				
Additional Personal Exemptions	1,144				

Hawaii allows you to double your personal exemption of you are over 65.

Property tax relief is available to seniors. It varies by county and by age. An additional credit is also available for homeowners 55 and older who earn less than $20,000.

Idaho

Idaho does not tax Social Security, railroad retirement or Canadian social security benefits. You also reduce federal civil service pension income, Idaho fireman pension income, policemen of an Idaho city pension income, and military pensions by the amount between your Social Security or railroad retirement and $41,814 (jointly) or $31,956 (individual).

Idaho Tax Brackets					
Single			Joint		
From	To	Rate	From	To	Rate
-	1,454	1.60%	-	2,908	1.60%
1,454	2,908	3.60%	2,908	5,816	3.60%
2,908	4,362	4.10%	5,816	8,724	4.10%
4,362	5,816	5.10%	8,724	11,632	5.10%
5,816	7,270	6.10%	11,632	14,540	6.10%
7,270	10,905	7.10%	14,540	21,810	7.10%
10,905	+	7.40%	21,810	+	7.40%
Standard Deduction Single	6,350				
Standard Deduction Joint	12,700				
Personal Exemption Single	4,050				
Personal Exemption Joint	8,100				
Additional Personal Exemptions	4,050				

Homeowner property taxes can be reduced by up to $1,320 for lower income taxpayers over 65.

Illinois

Illinois excludes a broad range of retirement income sources from state income taxation. You may exclude distributions from qualified retirement plans, government pensions and deferred compensation, Social Security, railroad retirement, military pensions and proceeds of redemption of U.S. retirement bonds.

Illinois has a flat income tax of 3.75% of federal taxable income, after the above adjustments. There are no standard deductions, and exemptions are $2,175 each.

Illinois is another state that offers property tax relief to seniors using a very complicated system.

Indiana

Social Security is exempt from taxation in Indiana. A deduction of up to $2,000 for those receiving federal civil service pension can be taken for taxpayers 62 and older. Military retirees 60 and older can deduct up to $5,000 of their military pension.

Indiana uses federal taxable income, after the above adjustments, to determine state taxable income, taxed at a flat rate of 3.3%.

Some property tax relief is available based on income and property value for those over 65.

Iowa

Up to $25,000 of Social Security ($32,000 for couples) is excluded from Iowa taxable income. All other retirement income is also excluded, up to $6,000 for individuals or $12,000 for joint filers, for those age 55 and older. You also can deduct your federal income taxes if you itemize.

Iowa Tax Brackets					
Single			Joint		
From	To	Rate	From	To	Rate
-	1,573	0.36%	-	1,573	0.36%
1,573	3,146	0.72%	1,573	3,146	0.72%
3,146	6,292	2.43%	3,146	6,292	2.43%
6,292	14,157	4.50%	6,292	14,157	4.50%
14,157	23,595	6.12%	14,157	23,595	6.12%
23,595	31,460	6.48%	23,595	31,460	6.48%
31,460	47,190	6.80%	31,460	47,190	6.80%
47,190	70,785	7.92%	47,190	70,785	7.92%
70,785	+	8.98%	70,785	+	8.98%
Standard Deduction Single	2,000				
Standard Deduction Joint	4,920				
Personal Exemption Single	40				
Personal Exemption Joint	80				
Additional Personal Exemptions	40				

A property tax credit of up to $4,850 is available for those with taxable income under $19,503 who are 65 and older.

Kansas

Military, federal civil service, Kansas/local pensions and railroad retirement are fully exempt from state income taxes. Social Security is exempt for residents with federal adjusted gross income of $75,000 or less. Out-of-state government pensions are fully taxed.

Kansas Tax Brackets					
Single			Joint		
From	To	Rate	From	To	Rate
-	15,000	2.90%	-	30,000	2.90%
15,000	30,000	4.90%	30,000	60,000	4.90%
30,000	+	5.20%	60,000	+	5.20%
Standard Deduction Single		3,000			
Standard Deduction Joint		7,500			
Personal Exemption Single		2,250			
Personal Exemption Joint		4,500			
Additional Personal Exemptions		2,250			

For taxpayers with taxable income of $17,700 or less who are at least 65, up to 45% of property taxes paid are refundable. Another property tax refund is also available of up to $700 under some conditions.

Kentucky

Social Security and railroad retirement are exempt from state income taxes. You can also exclude up to $41,110 for income from military, federal civil service, state/local government, qualified private pensions, and annuities.

Kentucky Tax Brackets					
Single			Joint		
From	To	Rate	From	To	Rate
-	3,000	2.00%	-	3,000	2.00%
3,000	4,000	3.00%	3,000	4,000	3.00%
4,000	5,000	4.00%	4,000	5,000	4.00%
5,000	8,000	5.00%	5,000	8,000	5.00%
8,000	75,000	5.80%	8,000	75,000	5.80%
75,000	+	6.00%	75,000	+	6.00%
Standard Deduction Single	2,480				
Standard Deduction Joint	2,480				
Personal Exemption Single	10				
Personal Exemption Joint	10				
Additional Personal Exemptions	10				

$34,000 of home value is exempt from property tax for taxpayers over 65.

Louisiana

Taxpayers 65 and older may exclude up to $6,000 of retirement income. Federal retirees may also exclude their pension income. In addition, deferred compensation from the municipal and state police employee's retirement is exempt from income tax.

Louisiana Tax Brackets					
Single			Joint		
From	To	Rate	From	To	Rate
-	12,500	2.00%	-	25,000	2.00%
12,500	50,000	4.00%	25,000	100,000	4.00%
50,000	+	6.00%	100,000	+	6.00%
Standard Deduction Single	-				
Standard Deduction Joint	-				
Personal Exemption Single	4,500				
Personal Exemption Joint	9,000				
Additional Personal Exemptions	1,000				

Federal income taxes can be deducted if deductions are itemized.

Taxpayers whose adjusted gross household income is less than $58,531 will have the value of their home frozen for tax purposes so their property taxes will not increase.

Maine

You may deduct up to $6,000 of eligible pension income, including Social Security and railroad retirement. Some retirement benefits have had the limit raised to $10,000.

Maine Tax Brackets					
Single			Joint		
From	To	Rate	From	To	Rate
-	21,050	5.80%	-	42,099	5.80%
21,050	50,000	6.75%	42,099	74,999	6.75%
50,000	+	7.15%	74,999	+	7.15%
Standard Deduction Single	11,600				
Standard Deduction Joint	23,200				
Personal Exemption Single	4,050				
Personal Exemption Joint	8,100				
Additional Personal Exemptions	4,050				

Maine offers a wide range of property tax relief programs for single taxpayers under $64,950 in income, $86,600 for joint filers. There is also a $750 property tax credit available for seniors who engage in volunteer service.

Maryland

Social Security and railroad retirement income are not taxed. A $27,100 pension exclusion is also available under certain conditions. Out-of-state government pensions do not qualify for the exclusion.

Maryland Tax Brackets					
Single			Joint		
From	To	Rate	From	To	Rate
-	1,000	2.00%	-	1,000	2.00%
1,000	2,000	3.00%	1,000	2,000	3.00%
2,000	3,000	4.00%	2,000	3,000	4.00%
3,000	100,000	4.75%	3,000	150,000	4.75%
100,000	125,000	5.00%	150,000	175,000	5.00%
125,000	150,000	5.25%	175,000	225,000	5.25%
150,000	250,000	5.50%	225,000	300,000	5.50%
250,000	+	5.75%	300,000	+	5.75%
Standard Deduction Single		2,000			
Standard Deduction Joint		4,000			
Personal Exemption Single		3,200			
Personal Exemption Joint		6,400			
Additional Personal Exemptions		3,200			

Maryland also allows you to double your personal exemption if you are over 65.

Homeowners can receive a credit if their property taxes exceed a fixed percentage of their gross income. Property owners 65 and older can defer increases in their property taxes, which becomes a tax lien on the property.

Massachusetts

Social Security, military, federal civil service and in-state state/local government pensions are exempt. Out-of-state pensions are also exempt if the states they are from do not tax Massachusetts pensions.

Massachusetts has a flat tax of 5.10%, with personal exemptions of $4,400 single, $8,800 joint and $1,000 for dependents. Taxpayers over 65 qualify for an additional $700 exemption.

No property tax relief for seniors is available.

Michigan

Social Security, military, federal, and state/local government pensions are exempt. Private pension income is exempt up to $47,309 (individual filers) or $94,618 (married filing jointly). These private pensions are reduced by the amount of any public pension deduction claimed. Taxpayers 65 or older may deduct interest, dividends, and capital gains up to $20,000 (individual filers) or $40,000 (married filing jointly). These deductions are reduced by any pension exemption taken. Federal and Michigan public pensions are totally exempt. Public pensions include benefits received from the federal civil service, state of Michigan public retirement systems and political subdivisions of Michigan, military retirement and tier 2 railroad retirement. If the conditions of the plan under step one are met, then these payments are totally exempt from Michigan income tax. Michigan residents can treat the public pensions received from the following states as totally exempt: Alaska, Florida, Hawaii, Illinois, Massachusetts, Mississippi, Nevada, New Hampshire, Pennsylvania, South Dakota, Tennessee, Texas, Washington, and Wyoming. Michigan residents who receive public pensions from other states are subject to the private pension exemption limits. Michigan residents who receive public pensions from states not listed above are subject to the private pension exemption limits.

Michigan has a flat tax rate of 4.25% of federal adjusted gross income, with some modifications.

Minnesota

Minnesota taxes Social Security and railroad retirement benefits to the same extent they are taxable on your federal return.

Minnesota Tax Brackets					
Single			Joint		
From	To	Rate	From	To	Rate
-	25,390	5.35%	-	37,110	5.35%
25,390	83,400	7.05%	37,110	147,450	7.05%
83,400	156,911	7.85%	147,450	261,510	7.85%
156,911	+	9.85%	261,510	+	9.85%
Standard Deduction Single		6,350			
Standard Deduction Joint		12,700			
Personal Exemption Single		4,050			
Personal Exemption Joint		8,100			
Additional Personal Exemptions		4,050			

Minnesota allows taxpayers with incomes under $60.000 to defer property taxes on their homes that exceed 3.00% of your total household income. The deferred amount is charged a low interest rate and is attached as a lien on the home.

Mississippi

All qualified retirement income is exempt from state income taxes.

Mississippi Tax Brackets						
Single			Joint			
From	To	Rate	From	To	Rate	
-	5,000	3.00%	-	5,000	3.00%	
5,000	10,000	4.00%	5,000	10,000	4.00%	
10,000	+	5.00%	10,000	+	5.00%	
Standard Deduction Single		2,300				
Standard Deduction Joint		4,600				
Personal Exemption Single		6,000				
Personal Exemption Joint		12,000				
Additional Personal Exemptions		1,500				

Missouri

Social Security benefits are deductible (not excluded). Some public pensions are exempt. Up to 15% of military pension is exempt, which will increase 15% each year until it becomes fully exempt.

Missouri Tax Brackets					
Single			Joint		
From	To	Rate	From	To	Rate
-	1,008	1.50%	-	1,008	1.50%
1,008	2,016	2.00%	1,008	2,016	2.00%
2,016	3,024	2.50%	2,016	3,024	2.50%
3,024	4,032	3.00%	3,024	4,032	3.00%
4,032	5,040	3.50%	4,032	5,040	3.50%
5,040	6,048	4.00%	5,040	6,048	4.00%
6,048	7,056	4.50%	6,048	7,056	4.50%
7,056	8,064	5.00%	7,056	8,064	5.00%
4,032	9,072	5.50%	4,032	9,072	5.50%
9,072	+	6.00%	9,072	+	6.00%
Standard Deduction Single	6,350				
Standard Deduction Joint	12,700				
Personal Exemption Single	2,100				
Personal Exemption Joint	4,200				
Additional Personal Exemptions	1,200				

Some income based property credit is available for some homeowners.

Montana

Tier I and tier II railroad retirement benefits are exempt. All other retirement income, including Social Security, is exempt up to $3,600 per individual, once certain income limits are met. Taxation of social security benefits may differ from your federal return based on a worksheet calculation.

Montana Tax Brackets						
Single			Joint			
From	To	Rate	From	To	Rate	
-	2,900	1.00%	-	2,900	1.00%	
2,900	5,200	2.00%	2,900	5,200	2.00%	
5,200	7,900	3.00%	5,200	7,900	3.00%	
7,900	10,600	4.00%	7,900	10,600	4.00%	
10,600	13,600	5.00%	10,600	13,600	5.00%	
13,600	17,600	6.00%	13,600	17,600	6.00%	
17,600	+	6.90%	17,600	+	6.90%	
Standard Deduction Single		4,510				
Standard Deduction Joint		9,020				
Personal Exemption Single		2,400				
Personal Exemption Joint		4,800				
Additional Personal Exemptions		2,400				

Montana property owners can have their property taxes reduced if they meet certain qualifications. Any homeowner or renter age 62 or over can apply for a credit if they have lived in Montana for 9 months, occupied a residence for 6 months, and had a gross household income of less than $45,000.

Nebraska

Only railroad retirement benefits are exempt. Social Security is taxed to the extent of federal taxation. Military benefits are partially exempt, either 40% of benefits for 7 years or 15% of benefits for life at the discretion of the taxpayer.

Nebraska Tax Brackets					
Single			Joint		
From	To	Rate	From	To	Rate
-	3,090	2.46%	-	5,170	2.46%
3,091	18,510	3.51%	5,171	37,030	3.51%
18,511	29,830	5.01%	37,031	59,660	5.01%
29,831	+	6.84%	59,661	+	6.84%
Standard Deduction Single		6,350			
Standard Deduction Joint		12,700			
Personal Exemption Single		132	Exemptions used as		
Personal Exemption Joint		264	credits.		
Additional Personal Exemptions		132			

Some property tax relief is available to seniors age 65 and older based on a complex set of criteria.

Nevada

There is no state income tax in Nevada. No property tax relief is available to seniors.

New Hampshire

State income tax is limited to a 5.00% tax on dividends of over $2,400 ($4,800 for joint filers). A $1,200 exemption is available to residents 65 and over.

A very limited property tax deferral is available to taxpayers who earn less than $3,000 ($6,000 joint).

New Jersey

Social Security, railroad retirement, total and permanent disability pensions, and military pensions are excluded. For taxpayers 62 and older whose gross income, before pension deductions, does not exceed $100,000, up to $20,000 (joint) of pensions and IRA distributions can be excluded.

New Jersey Tax Brackets					
Single			Joint		
From	To	Rate	From	To	Rate
-	20,000	1.40%	-	20,000	1.40%
20,000	35,000	1.75%	20,000	50,000	1.75%
35,000	40,000	3.50%	50,000	70,000	2.45%
40,000	75,000	5.53%	70,000	80,000	3.50%
75,000	500,000	6.37%	80,000	150,000	5.53%
500,000	+	8.97%	150,000	500,000	6.37%
			500,000	+	8.97%
Standard Deduction Single	-				
Standard Deduction Joint	-				
Personal Exemption Single	1,000				
Personal Exemption Joint	2,000				
Additional Personal Exemptions	1,500				

Taxpayers over 65 can deduct up to $250 of their property taxes.

New Mexico

A $2,500 exclusion is available for taxpayer with income under $36,667 (single) and $55,000 (joint). A deduction is also available if single income is under $28,500; $51,000 joint.

New Mexico Tax Brackets					
Single			Joint		
From	To	Rate	From	To	Rate
-	5,500	1.70%	-	8,000	1.70%
5,500	11,000	3.20%	8,000	16,000	3.20%
11,000	16,000	4.70%	16,000	24,000	4.70%
16,000	+	4.90%	24,000	+	4.90%
Standard Deduction Single	6,350				
Standard Deduction Joint	12,700				
Personal Exemption Single	4,050				
Personal Exemption Joint	8,100				
Additional Personal Exemptions	4,050				

A property tax rebate is available for homeowners with gross income under $18,000.

New York

Social Security, federal civil service, New York state/local government pensions are exempt. Up to $20,000 of private and out-of-state government pensions are also exempt.

New York Tax Brackets					
Single			Joint		
From	To	Rate	From	To	Rate
-	8,500	4.00%	-	17,150	4.00%
8,500	11,700	4.50%	17,150	23,600	4.50%
11,700	13,900	5.25%	23,600	27,900	5.25%
13,900	21,400	5.90%	27,900	43,000	5.90%
21,400	80,650	6.45%	43,000	161,550	6.45%
80,650	215,400	6.65%	161,550	323,200	6.65%
215,400	1,077,550	6.85%	323,200	2,155,350	6.85%
1,077,550	+	8.82%	2,155,350	+	8.82%
Standard Deduction Single		8,000			
Standard Deduction Joint		16,050			
Personal Exemption Single		-			
Personal Exemption Joint		-			
Additional Personal Exemptions		1,000			

Property tax relief to seniors is at the option of local governments and public school districts.

North Carolina

Social Security is exempt from state income taxes. Up to 100% of military pensions and state retirees may be exempt, based on length of service. Those who don't meet the qualifications for the full exemption can exempt up to $4,000.

The North Carolina income tax rate is flat at 5.75%, with a standard deduction of $8,750 for single taxpayers and $17,500 for joint filers.

Some homeowners can receive minor property tax relief based on income criteria.

North Dakota

Up to $5,000 of pension, after deducting Social Security can be excluded.

North Dakota Tax Brackets					
Single			Joint		
From	To	Rate	From	To	Rate
-	37,950	1.10%	-	63,400	1.10%
37,950	91,900	2.04%	63,400	153,100	2.04%
91,900	191,650	2.27%	153,100	233,350	2.27%
191,650	416,700	2.64%	233,350	416,700	2.64%
416,700	+	2.90%	416,700	+	2.90%
Standard Deduction Single	6,350				
Standard Deduction Joint	12,700				
Personal Exemption Single	4,050				
Personal Exemption Joint	8,100				
Additional Personal Exemptions	4,050				

A maximum homestead credit of $4,500 is available for seniors with assets under $75,000 and income under $18,000.

Ohio

Social Security and railroad retirement benefits are exempt from state taxations. A small $50 credit is available for seniors 65 and over.

Ohio Tax Brackets					
Single			Joint		
From	To	Rate	From	To	Rate
-	5,250	0.50%	-	5,250	0.50%
5,250	10,500	0.99%	5,250	10,500	0.99%
10,500	15,800	1.98%	10,500	15,800	1.98%
15,800	21,100	2.48%	15,800	21,100	2.48%
21,100	42,100	2.97%	21,100	42,100	2.97%
42,100	84,200	3.46%	42,100	84,200	3.46%
84,200	105,300	3.96%	84,200	105,300	3.96%
105,300	210,600	4.60%	105,300	210,600	4.60%
210,600	+	5.00%	210,600	+	5.00%
Standard Deduction Single	-				
Standard Deduction Joint	-				
Personal Exemption Single	2,250				
Personal Exemption Joint	4,500				
Additional Personal Exemptions	2,250				

A homestead exemption if available for homeowners 65 and over. The average reduction in taxes for 2010 was $441 per household.

Oklahoma

Social Security is exempt from taxation. Each individual may also exclude up to $10,000 of retirement income from pension plans and qualified plans. Up to 75% of military benefits can be used to reach the $10,000 limit.

Oklahoma Tax Brackets					
Single			Joint		
From	To	Rate	From	To	Rate
-	1,000	0.50%	-	2,000	0.50%
1,000	2,500	1.00%	2,000	5,000	1.00%
2,500	3,750	2.00%	5,000	7,500	2.00%
3,750	4,900	3.00%	7,500	9,800	3.00%
4,900	7,200	4.00%	9,800	12,200	4.00%
7,200	+	5.00%	12,200	+	5.00%
Standard Deduction Single	6,350				
Standard Deduction Joint	12,700				
Personal Exemption Single	1,000				
Personal Exemption Joint	2,000				
Additional Personal Exemptions	1,000				

Oklahoma allows taxpayers over 65 to double their exemption.

A property tax refund is available to taxpayers 65 and older with income less than $12,000.

Oregon

Social Security and railroad retirement is exempt from state taxation. Some federal and military pension recipients may also exclude their pensions based on dates of service.

Oregon Tax Brackets					
Single			Joint		
From	To	Rate	From	To	Rate
-	3,350	5.00%	-	6,700	5.00%
3,350	8,400	7.00%	6,700	16,900	7.00%
8,400	125,000	9.00%	16,900	250,000	9.00%
125,000	+	9.90%	250,000	+	9.90%
Standard Deduction Single		2,155			
Standard Deduction Joint		4,310			
Personal Exemption Single		195			
Personal Exemption Joint		390			
Additional Personal Exemptions		195			

Oregon allows you to double your exemption if you are over 65.

Property taxes may be deferred. Deferred taxes are paid when the owner dies, sells the property or moves out. Deferred taxes are charged 6% simple interest. The deferral is available if household income is less than $39,500.

Pennsylvania

Social Security, railroad retirement, and all other retirement is not taxed after age 59 ½, provided the person has reached retirement based on years of service.

Income is taxed at a flat rate of 3.07%.

For households with income under $35,000, a rebate of up to $975 is available. To qualify for the limit, one half of Social Security and railroad retirement can be excluded.

Rhode Island

Only railroad retirement benefits are exempt. Social Security is taxed to the extent it is federally taxed.

Rhode Island Tax Brackets					
Single			Joint		
From	To	Rate	From	To	Rate
-	61,300	3.75%	-	61,300	3.75%
61,300	139,400	4.75%	61,300	139,400	4.75%
139,400	+	5.99%	139,400	+	5.99%
Standard Deduction Single	8,375				
Standard Deduction Joint	16,750				
Personal Exemption Single	3,900				
Personal Exemption Joint	7,800				
Additional Personal Exemptions	3,900				

Taxpayers over 65 can double their exemption.

Homeowners who are 65 and older, and earn under $30,000, can get a property tax relief credit of up to $300.

South Carolina

Social Security is exempt from state income tax. Taxpayers 65 and older can exempt up to $15,000 of retirement income. Military retirees with at least 20 years of service can deduct up to $3,000 until age 65; the deduction moves up to $10,000 at 65.

South Carolina Tax Brackets					
Single			Joint		
From	To	Rate	From	To	Rate
-	2,930	0.00%	-	2,930	0.00%
2,930	5,860	3.00%	2,930	5,860	3.00%
5,860	8,790	4.00%	5,860	8,790	4.00%
8,790	11,720	5.00%	8,790	11,720	5.00%
11,720	14,650	6.00%	11,720	14,650	6.00%
14,650	+	7.00%	14,650	+	7.00%
Standard Deduction Single	6,350				
Standard Deduction Joint	12,700				
Personal Exemption Single	4,050				
Personal Exemption Joint	8,100				
Additional Personal Exemptions	4,050				

The personal exemption is doubled for taxpayers 65 and older.

Homeowners 65 and older can exempt up to $50,000 equity of their personal residence from property taxes.

South Dakota

There is no personal income tax in South Dakota.

The state has a wide range of property tax relief programs available, primarily for low income residents.

Tennessee

Salaries, wages, Social Security, qualified plan distributions, and pension income are not taxed. A 6% tax is levied on stock dividends and interest income. The first $1,250 per tax payer is exempt. The exemption increases to $26,000 (single) and $27,000 (joint) for taxpayers 65 and over.

Very minimal personal property tax relief is available for low income homeowners.

Texas

There is no personal income tax in Texas.

Homeowners 65 and older receive a $10,000 homestead exemption from property tax, in addition to the $15,000 homestead exemption everyone qualifies for. Once qualified, the homeowner's school taxes are frozen unless improvements to the property are made.

Utah

A credit of up to $450 per taxpayer is available for taxpayers 65 and over, subject to income limits.

Utah has a flat income tax of 5%, after personal exemptions of $3,038 each.

Homeowners 65 and older, with household income under $29,210 can receive a property tax credit of up to $865.

Vermont

Railroad retirement is the only retirement income exclude from state income taxation.

Vermont Tax Brackets					
Single			Joint		
From	To	Rate	From	To	Rate
-	37,950	3.55%	-	63,350	3.55%
37,950	91,900	6.80%	63,350	153,100	6.80%
91,900	191,650	7.80%	153,100	233,350	7.80%
191,650	416,700	8.80%	233,350	416,700	8.80%
416,700	+	8.95%	416,700	+	8.95%
Standard Deduction Single	6,350				
Standard Deduction Joint	12,700				
Personal Exemption Single	4,050				
Personal Exemption Joint	8,100				
Additional Personal Exemptions	4,050				

No property tax relief is available for seniors.

Virginia

Social Security and railroad retirement is exempt from taxation. Other retirement income can be deducted, up to $6,000 per person at 64, increasing to $12,000 for those 65 and older.

Virginia Tax Brackets					
Single			Joint		
From	To	Rate	From	To	Rate
-	3,000	2.00%	-	3,000	2.00%
3,000	5,000	3.00%	3,000	5,000	3.00%
5,000	17,000	5.00%	5,000	17,000	5.00%
17,000	+	5.75%	17,000	+	5.75%
Standard Deduction Single		3,000			
Standard Deduction Joint		6,000			
Personal Exemption Single		930			
Personal Exemption Joint		1,860			
Additional Personal Exemptions		930			

A county, city, or town may enact a property tax relief program for senior citizens 65 and older with income under $50,000.

Washington

There is no personal income tax in Washington.

Homeowners with income under $35,000 may qualify for a tax deferral program. You may also be exempt from levies.

West Virginia

Social Security is taxed to the same extent it is taxed at the federal level. Taxpayers over 65 can exclude up to $8,000 cumulatively from any retirement income sources. Participants in the WV Teachers Retirement System, WV Employees Retirement System, and military or federal retirement systems can exclude $2,000 at any age.

West Virginia Tax Brackets						
Single			Joint			
From	To	Rate	From	To	Rate	
-	10,000	3.00%	-	10,000	3.00%	
10,000	25,000	4.00%	10,000	25,000	4.00%	
25,000	40,000	4.50%	25,000	40,000	4.50%	
40,000	60,000	6.00%	40,000	60,000	6.00%	
60,000	+	6.50%	60,000	+	6.50%	
Standard Deduction Single	-					
Standard Deduction Joint	-					
Personal Exemption Single	2,000					
Personal Exemption Joint	4,000					
Additional Personal Exemptions	2,000					

Homeowners 65 and older may qualify for a property tax credit of up to $1,000.

Wisconsin

Social Security and railroad retirement are exempt from taxation. Military retirement is exempt. Lower income residents 65 and older can also exclude up to $5,000 of retirement benefits if their federal adjusted gross income s under $30,000 ($15,000 single).

Wiscosin Tax Brackets					
Single			Joint		
From	To	Rate	From	To	Rate
-	11,230	4.00%	-	14,980	4.00%
11,230	22,470	5.84%	14,980	29,960	5.84%
22,470	247,350	6.27%	29,960	329,810	6.27%
247,350	+	7.65%	329,810	+	7.65%
Standard Deduction Single	10,380				
Standard Deduction Joint	19,210				
Personal Exemption Single	700				
Personal Exemption Joint	1,400				
Additional Personal Exemptions	1,400				

Homeowners with income under $24,680 can receive a credit against income taxes at any age.

Wyoming

Wyoming has no personal income tax.

The state has several property tax relief, credit, and deferral programs based on income.

Glossary of Common Terms

Adjusted Gross Income	Total gross income minus specific deductions.
Alternative Minimum Tax	A supplemental income tax imposed by the federal government, required in addition to the baseline income tax on certain individuals that have exemptions or special circumstances allowing for lower payments of the standard income tax.
Annuity	A fixed sum of money paid to someone each year, typically for the rest of their life or a form of insurance entitling the investor to a series of annual amounts either immediately or sometime in the future.
Beneficiary	The person named to inherit an IRA or to receive the death benefit of a life insurance policy.
Beneficiary IRA	An IRA that was inherited from someone else.
Capital Asset	Significant pieces of property such as homes, cars, investment properties, stocks, bonds and even collectibles. For businesses, a capital asset is a type of asset with a useful life longer than a year that is not intended for sale in the regular course of the business's operation.
Charitable Remainder Trust	A split interest trust. Typically, a donor will place in the trust a capital asset that is then sold to be reinvested in income oriented securities. The donor receives the income and a charity receives the remainder of the

trust balance at the end of the donor's life.

Cost Basis

The amount paid for a capital asset, adjusted upwards for improvements and downwards for depreciation taken or allowed.

CPA

Certified Public Accountant. A person trained in financial issues, typically taxes.

Deduction

A reduction from gross income.

Depreciation

A reduction in a capital asset's value, typically spread over the useful life of the asset.

Direct Rollover

The movement of the balance of a qualified retirement plan or IRA from one custodian to another.

Early Withdrawal Penalty

The penalty for taking distributions from an IRA prior to reaching age 59 ½ (55 for a company sponsored plan) when no exceptions to the penalty have been met. The penalty is typically 10% of the amount withdrawn.

Enrolled Agent

A tax professional who has completed training and passed a competency test who is certified to give tax advice and file income tax returns.

Estate

The value of a person's holdings. An estate can include a home, investments, personal assets, and shares of business interests.

Exclusion

A cash flow that is not included in gross income.

Exemption

Similar to an exclusion, usually not taxed, but may be reportable.

FICA Withholding

The amount withheld from wages (6.2%)

and self-employment income (12.4%) used to fund Social Security retirement and disability programs.

Gross Income

Income before deductions and exemptions.

Home Equity

The difference between the value of a home and the mortgage balance.

Indirect Rollover

The movement on a retirement account balance by which the owner of the account takes receipt of the funds before depositing the funds with a different custodian.

IRA

Individual retirement arrangement. An account that, generally, has deductible contributions. Withdrawals are taxable, except in the case of Roth IRAs.

Irrevocable Trust

An entity established by a donor (grantor) in which assets are irrevocably gifted to the entity. The grantor may have access to the trust income and possibly some principle, but cannot take back the assets placed in the trust.

Itemized Deductions

Expenses that the IRS allows you to reduce your gross income. Typical deductions include health insurance expenses, home mortgage interest, taxes, and charitable contributions.

Joint Tenancy

A type of ownership of an asset in which all joint owners own an equal share of the asset. At one owner's death, the remaining owner(s) equal split the assets equally.

Legacy

What a person leaves behind when he passes away. Can refer to assets as well as their contribution to their family or to society.

Living Trust	Also referred to as a revocable trust. A trust that can be changed or liquidated at any time. When properly funded and structured, can determine how to settle an estate without the need of probate.
Medicare Withholding	The amount withheld from wages (1.45%) and self-employment earnings (2.90%) used to fund the Medicare insurance system that provides part of the health insurance needed by people over 65.
Modified Adj. Gross Income	MAGI is used as a basis for determining whether you qualify for certain tax deductions. It is calculated by applying to adjusted gross income several deductions such as student loan interest, one half of self-employment tax, passive losses or income, IRA contributions, taxable Social Security, etc.
Modified Endowment Contract	A type of life insurance policy that one typically purchases with on upfront payment. Unlike traditional cash value permanent life insurance, tax free loans are not available.
Municipal Bonds	Bonds issued by states, counties, and cities as well as some private business that are funding special purpose projects. Typically, the interest it not taxable on the federal level and also not taxable in the state wherein the municipality is located.
Net Unrealized Appreciation	The difference in the price paid for a company stock held in a qualified retirement plan and the current value of the stock.
Non-Qualified Annuity	An annuity outside of a qualified plan; an annuity funded with after tax funds.

Personal Exemptions	The amount the federal or state government allows you to reduce your adjusted gross income by in order to determine your taxable income.
Primary Insurance Amount	Your monthly Social Security benefit at your full retirement age—currently age 66.
Probate	The court directed process of accounting for the assets of a deceased person and distributing those assets to heirs—either based on instructions in a will left by the deceased or by the state's order or precedent.
Provisional Income	The amount used to determine how much of your social security will be taxed. It equals adjusted gross income + one half of your Social Security + plus tax exempt income from municipal bonds.
Qualified Annuity	An annuity held with some type of tax qualified plan, such as an IRA or company sponsored retirement plan.
Qualified Charitable Distribution	A distribution of a person's required minimum distribution that goes directly to a charity. The amount of the distribution is excluded from gross income
Qualified Dividends	Dividends paid by, primarily, U.S. based companies that receive preferential tax treatment; they are taxed the same as capital gains.
Railroad Retirement	A precursor to the Social Security system, that was designed to provide railroad employees a supplemental retirement income.
Required Minimum Distribution	The annual amount you must distribute from your IRA once you reach age 70 ½ or the amount you must distribute from a

beneficiary IRA beginning the year after death.

Reverse Mortgage	An arrangement in which a mortgage companies provides payments—or establish a line of credit for you in exchange for receiving equity in your home when you die equal to the amount of payments made to you.
Roth Conversion	The process of converting a traditional IRA to a Roth IRA in an attempt to reduce one's own taxes or the taxes of an heir who will inherit the IRA.
Roth IRA	A tax-deferred account in which no deduction is taken when deposits are made. Provided certain conditions are met, distributions are tax free.
Standard Deduction	The amount a taxpayer is allowed to deduct if one does not have sufficient itemized deductions to reach the level of the standard deduction.
Taxable Income	The amount of your income, after deductions, exemptions and modifications that taxes are paid on.
Tenants in Common	A way of owning an asset jointly. Unlike joint tenancy, when one tenant passes way, their ownership is included in their estate —the remaining tenants do not get an equal share.
Term Life Insurance	Life insurance that expires after a certain period of time.
Transfer on Death	Also sometimes referred to a *payment on death*. A contractual specification placed on an asset that allows the asset to pass free of probate to an heir.

Whole Life Insurance   Life insurance designed to provide coverage the entire life of a policy holder.

ABOUT THE AUTHOR

After receiving his Bachelor of Science degree in Accounting from the University of Wyoming in 1988, Bruce Larsen started his professional career as a corporate controller in Billings, Montana. Wanting interface with people, rather than computers, Bruce left accounting in 1998 and began a financial advisory career, the career he currently practices. An adjunct to serving clients, Bruce actively tracks evolutions in financial systems design to keep pace with the continually changing regulatory environment—including tax changes—which in sum auspices this book.

Bruce is married to Cindy. Bruce and Cindy reside in Denver, Colorado with two pre-twenties children, Virginia and Charles.

Made in the USA
Columbia, SC
27 February 2018